Physical Characteristics
Australian Kelpie
(from the Working Kelpie Council of Australia)

Color: Any color and markings historically associated with the development of the breed.

Tail: When viewed from the side the butt of the tail should be well let down.

Hindquarters: Should show breadth and strength with the rump rather long and sloping. When viewed from the side, the overall upper line of the rump and tail should form a smooth curve when the dog is standing at rest.

Size: Classified as a medium-sized dog.

Coat: Moderately short, flat, straight and weather-resisting outer coat, with or without a short dense undercoat.

Hind Feet: Slightly elongated in comparison with the front feet.

Australian Kelpie

By Charlotte Schwartz

Contents

Training Your Australian Kelpie 82

Begin with the basics of training the puppy and adult dog. Learn the principles of house-training the Australian Kelpie, including the use of crates. Get started by introducing the pup to his collar and leash, and progress to the basic commands and herding training. Find out about obedience classes and other activities.

Healthcare of Your Australian Kelpie 115

By Lowell Ackerman DVM, DACVD
Become your dog's healthcare advocate and a well-educated canine keeper. Select a skilled and able veterinarian. Discuss pet insurance, vaccinations and infectious diseases, the neuter/spay decision, parasite control and breed-specific health concerns.

Your Senior Australian Kelpie 142

Know when to consider your Australian Kelpie a senior and what special needs he will have. Learn to recognize the signs of aging in terms of physical and behavioral traits and what your vet can do to optimize your dog's golden years.

Behavior of Your Australian Kelpie 146

Analyze the canine mind to understand what makes your Australian Kelpie tick. The following potential problems are addressed: aggression (fear biting, inter-canine and dominant), sexual misconduct, chewing, digging, jumping up and barking.

KENNEL CLUB BOOKS® AUSTRALIAN KELPIE
ISBN: 1-59378-369-8

Copyright © 2007 • Kennel Club Books, LLC • 308 Main Street, Allenhurst, NJ 07711 USA
Cover Design Patented: US 6,435,559 B2 • Printed in South Korea

Library of Congress Cataloging-in-Publication Data
Schwartz, Charlotte.
  Australian kelpie / by Charlotte Schwartz.
      p. cm. 1593783698
1. Australian kelpie. I. Title.

SF429.A78S39 2007
636.737--dc22   2006016294

10 9 8 7 6 5 4 3 2 1

Photography by Michael Trafford
with additional photographs contributed by:

Paulette Braun, Alan and Sandy Carey, Carolina Biological Supply, Tony Dixon, Donna Dunham, W. P. Fleming/Viesti Associates, Isabelle Français, Carol Ann Johnson, Bill Jonas, Sven Karlsson, Dr. Dennis Kunkel, Tam C. Nguyen, Phototake, Jean Claude Revy, Judith Selby, Diane Stark, Roger Urricelquis and Alice van Kempen.

Illustrations by Patricia Peters.

The Australian Kelpie is a medium-sized, hardy and alert working dog whose intelligence and skills have won him the admiration of stockmen around the world.

HISTORY OF THE

AUSTRALIAN KELPIE

It was early morning and the horizon barely hinted at the coming dawn. Two small children, still dressed in pajamas, sat on the floor playing with a set of wooden blocks. Nearby, their mother made a pot of coffee and prepared bowls of breakfast cereal.

On an oval rug near the children, a dark brown dog, medium in size with a pointed muzzle and a bushy tail, watched the children at play. Looking very much like an oversized fox, the dog rested his chin on his front paws as if studying the formation of the children's blocks.

Suddenly, a tall, mustached man with chestnut hair entered the room. Immediately, the dog got up, wagged his tail and went to his master. The children looked up at the man as he stood admiring the block structure.

"G'day, children. Look, Mum's got your brekkie on the table. Come. Get into your chairs."

After breakfast, the man glanced down at the dog sleeping beside him and said, "Come on, Hank. We've got to move those sheep to the upper hill pasture. And those cows need to be brought up to the barn for dusting."

A short time later, Hank, his tail wagging and a bright gleam of anticipation in his eyes, jumped into the utility truck alongside the man. They would spend the next eight to ten hours together, moving animal stock, patrolling the large property of the Goolong Ranch and working to maintain their part of Australia's sheep industry.

At day's end, Hank would return to the house with his master, eat his dinner, check out the children and sleep on a blanket next to his master's bed. If a stranger should approach the house, the dog, with his exceptional hearing, would alert his master and run to the children's room to make sure they were safe.

A typical Australian Kelpie, Hank would spend his life working with his owner, protecting his home and family and serving as a well-loved companion to the entire family. This is the life that makes the Kelpie content. Hank is a happy dog.

The Kelpie is a medium-sized dog with a short, coarse, weather-resistant outer coat and a broad

PHOTO COURTESY OF W. P. FLEMING/ VESTI ASSOCIATES.

head that tapers to a pointed, fox-like muzzle. A a soft undercoat helps to keep him cool in the Australian summer and warm in the winter. His color can range from black—these Kelpies are known as "Barbs"—to black and tan, red, chestnut brown or bluish gray.

Kelpies in North America stand somewhere between 17–23 inches at the shoulder on the average, with females at the smaller end of the spectrum and males at the larger. Average weight is 26–36 pounds for females and 35–45 pounds for males, although both height and weight can vary considerably, as Kelpies larger than this do exist. However, many breeders feel that height and weight are minor concerns if the dog is sound, in good shape and skilled at his work.

The Kelpie ideally has upright prick ears and a long, full, bushy tail. The Kelpie is a dog that looks a lot like a number of other breeds of dog. For example, he resembles the Dingo, the wild dog of Australia, the Border Collie and the larger Smooth Collie. The reason? All of these breeds were used in the creation of the Kelpie. There may also by other breeds whose contributions to the Kelpie have been lost in antiquity.

The breed's history began back

in the mid-1800s when two dogs were imported to Australia from Scotland. The dogs were Smooth Collies and were intended to be used as herders in the fast-growing Australian sheep industry. Back in those early times, when the outback was opening up to sheep-raising and ranch properties were often thousands of acres in size, it became apparent that men alone could not do the job of droving thousands of sheep. They needed dogs to help herd the stock.

Local dogs didn't have the stamina or physical ability to cope with the heat of the outback or the long hours and great distances necessary to manage these large flocks. Thus stockmen looked to Scotland, where rough mountainous terrain and severe weather conditions didn't bother the Collies that herded Scottish goats and sheep.

The two imported Collies were black and tan, with prick ears. They were imported into New South Wales around 1870 by George Robertson. One was a female named Jennie, the other a male called Brutus. A mating of the two dogs produced a dog named Caesar.

About the same time, a Mr. Jack Gleeson acquired a black and tan female pup bred by Mr. Robertson. He named her Kelpie, a Gaelic word meaning "watersprite." Gleeson also acquired a black, prick-eared male

named Moss from his friend, Mark Tully.

Eventually, Caesar was bred to Kelpie. One of the puppies from that union produced a black and tan female named King's Kelpie by her owner Mr. Charles King. The word "kelpie" seemed to be catching on, and henceforth all of the good herding dogs from subsequent litters were known as Kelpies.

One of Caesar's littermates, a dog named Laddie, was eventually bred to King's Kelpie. That mating produced a female named Sallie who was later bred to Moss. One of the puppies in that litter was a solid black dog that was called Barb, named after a black horse that won the prestigious Melbourne Cup in 1869. From that time on, all black Kelpies were known as Barbs.

Kelpie, Jack Gleeson's female, also became a famous sheepdog-trial winner. At just one year of age, she ran in her first trial and won easily. Her sensational win brought her fame and Gleeson a great demand for Kelpie's puppies. Everyone, it seemed, wanted a "Kelpie" pup; so from the late 1870s, the breed officially became known as the Australian Kelpie.

Sheep farmers and drovers alike admired Kelpies right from those early days of the Australian sheep industry's expansion. Kelpies were recognized for their working ability both in the outback and in sheep yards, as well as for their

The Australian Kelpie and Dingo were among the breeds featured on Australian postage stamps honoring the country's native dogs.

Like its Kelpie predecessor, the Australian Cattle Dog was developed to be a rugged, independent-thinking, dependable worker.

intelligence, compact build, athletic ability and devotion to their masters. As a matter of fact, the Kelpie was the last breed used in the development of the Australian Cattle Dog. The ideal characteristics of the Kelpie contributed the final traits necessary in the creation of a larger herding dog developed to move and control cattle.

Finally, in 1902, Robert Kaleski, a journalist and dog fancier devoted to Kelpies and Australian Cattle Dogs, wrote the standards for both breeds and presented them to the Cattle and Sheepdog Club of Australia and the Kennel Club of New South Wales. Both standards were approved in 1903, thus making these breeds officially recognized breeds in Australia.

The Australian Kelpie's

exportation to other countries around the world was inevitable. By the early 1900s, Kelpies were imported into the United States. Used to herd sheep in the western and southeastern states, the Kelpie proved its adaptability to various types of terrain and weather conditions, including the heat and humidity of the deep South. In 1941, Kelpies were admitted into the Miscellaneous Class of the American Kennel Club (AKC) and were approved for showing in conformation shows. However, the breed is no longer affiliated with the AKC and not eligible for AKC events.

Working ability is the main focus for Kelpie breeders, not conformation showing or other competitive events. While a breed

A cozy bed, a sturdy chew and the people he loves make the Kelpie a happy dog after a long day on the job.

standard does exist, a Kelpie's instinct with livestock is far more important than his adherence to specifications with regards to looks. Therefore, breeders concentrate on working ability in their breeding programs rather than on beauty points and ability for competitive dog sports. Working Kelpie "shows" are trials in which the dogs' abilities with livestock are judged—that's what makes a dog top-quality in this breed!

Today there are two versions of the Kelpie; in Australia, these versions are considered to be completely separate varieties since they differ from each other so much. The show-type Australian Kelpie is the variety seen in confor-mation shows, while the working Kelpie is the original variety still used as a working dog. Working dogs are registered in Australia with the Working Kelpie Council, while the show types are registered with the Australian National Kennel Council.

In North America, working Kelpies are registered by the North American Australian Kelpie Registry and the National Stock Dog Registry, as well as Australia's Working Kelpie Council. Working Kelpies, Inc. (WKI) is the national club for the breed in the US. This club's goal is to preserve the breed's herding and working instincts rather than to promote conforma-tion showing. In WKI events, dogs are judged based on their abilities with livestock and their adaptability to different working conditions, not on how close they come to a physical ideal. Those interested in the breed should visit www.kelpiesinc.com on the Internet for more information about the Kelpie in North America.

Since the late 1900s, Kelpies have been exported from Australia into such countries as New Caledonia, Argentina, Sweden, Italy, Canada and South Korea. Now recognized internationally as an indispensable addition to the livestock industry, the Australian Kelpie is assured respect and admiration from stockmen and drovers around the world.

CANIS LUPUS

"Grandma, what big teeth you have!" The gray wolf, a familiar figure in fairy tales and legends, has had its reputation tarnished and its population pummeled over the centuries. Yet it is the descendants of this much-feared creature to which we open our homes and hearts. Our beloved dog, *Canis domesticus*, derives directly from the gray wolf, a highly social canine that lives in elaborately structured packs. In the wild, the gray wolf can range from 60 to 175 pounds, standing between 25 and 40 inches in height.

CHARACTERISTICS OF THE

AUSTRALIAN KELPIE

The characteristics of a particular breed of dog give an overall picture of what the breed is like. Unlike the breed standard, which details the temperament and physical qualities that make the breed what it is, discussing the characteristics of a particular breed is a little more personal. For example, a breed may have a certain facial expression that makes it unique among all other breeds. Characteristics also include how the dog acts. The breed's tendency to behave in certain ways in certain situations helps to define that breed and sets it apart from other breeds, especially similar breeds.

For example, in describing a Beagle, one would mention how the dog keeps his nose close to the ground to sniff out his prey. A Miniature Schnauzer may be described as having a tendency to bark either in excitement or as a warning of someone's or something's approach. These are essential breed characteristics and important information for those seeking just the right breed for their lifestyle.

In the case of the Kelpie, detailing breed characteristics helps to distinguish it from other similar Australian working dogs. For example, most Kelpie owners who are also familiar with other working dogs find Kelpies particularly fond of children. They will tolerate a very young child's clinging to them, pulling on their ears and tails or even leaning on them as the child learns to walk. As for petting, most Kelpies are not "lap dogs," but the degree to which they enjoy petting and cuddling varies from dog to dog.

A true medium-sized dog with prick ears, a wedge-shaped head, a long tail with a "brush" at the end and a low-maintenance coat, the Kelpie will fit into an appropriate home life as well as farm life. Kelpies are playful and fun-loving. They are also athletic, intelligent, courageous and extremely alert. Constantly aware of what's going on around them, they are quiet companions yet brave and very protective when necessary. They are not guard dogs, but they are usually suspicious of strangers, remaining alert to activities around them and constantly watching their owners for signs of approval toward newcomers. Absent those signs of approval, the dog will defend his master and family with his life.

On the job, he is always eager to work and anxious to please. While he is an independent thinker, he does develop a good working relationship with a master who has established himself as the boss. Kelpies are much sought after by sheep farmers because they are noted for not pulling out wool or biting the sheep when working the flock. Pulling and biting are extremely undesirable traits in herding dogs and can prove costly to the farmer and painful to the sheep.

Some Kelpies are used for droving yearling cattle. In the US and Australia, they are known to ride atop the fuel tanks of their masters' motorcycles as they round up the herds and drive them to new pastures. Once at the new grazing sites, the Kelpies jump off the bikes and race around behind the cattle to move them as one unit through gates and fencing into the pastures.

When used as sheep herders, some Kelpies will jump up onto the backs of the sheep to move them along. This behavior seems

Although working ability is valued over beauty points in this breed, the Kelpie does have a range of striking colors, including solid black and all shades of red.

innate in some Kelpies while totally absent in others; it is not a behavior that can be taught. A dog either rides the backs of sheep or he doesn't. Either way, he moves the herd efficiently and with seemingly little effort.

While we are on the subject of herding, let us mention again that the Kelpie is a herding breed. In a pet home, this can translate to the Kelpie's viewing everyone and everything as part of his flock. Some Kelpies nip while herding, and this behavior appears in the pet home, too. The dog can be trained not to nip, but he can't be trained not to herd! Pet owners must put their dogs' safety foremost, realizing that a Kelpie will be off and running after anything that he thinks needs "rounding up," which can be dangerous. Intense herding

STOCKDOG CLUBS

In addition to Working Kelpies, Inc., there are specialty stockdog clubs throughout the US, such as the Red River Cattle Dog Association and the Western Cowdog Association. These associations are open to all breeds used to work livestock, and they promote the development of the dogs' natural abilities through competitions, trials, educational activities and training programs. The WKI's website (www.kelpiesinc.com) is a wonderful source of information on the breed and links to other clubs, organizations and points of interest for those dedicated to the working stockdog.

instincts are bred into this dog, which is why the Kelpie is such a wonderful working dog but is typically a less-than-ideal pet.

The active and independent-minded Kelpie likewise is affectionate and enjoys attention from the owners to which he is so loyal.

Being a highly intelligent and independent breed, the Kelpie is able to think on his own. For this reason, the breed is not highly successful in sports like obedience, freestyle, etc., which require repetition. The Kelpie seems to wonder why he has to do the same thing over and over again. His independence means that he will travel far to retrieve a stray cow or sheep, not tiring or giving up until the job is done. While this is a great benefit to the farmer, it is not a desirable quality in a pet dog.

While the Kelpie obviously is on his own when working, he should not just be "left loose" at other times. Usually Kelpies are kept in secure kennel runs or fenced areas when not working or inside the home with the family.

There are many books written by farmers and drovers about their working dogs. Many of the stories in these books are about the unique devotion, endurance and courage of Kelpies who have made a difference in the lives of the writers.

Take Jip, for example. A solid black Kelpie, Jip often moved a flock of sheep all by himself from one farm property to another while the farmer did other chores. The distance between the two properties was a little more than 4 miles. Once Jip got the flock moving, the farmer would call ahead to his other farm and arrange to have someone open the paddock gate for Jip. Once the dog moved the sheep into the paddock, he'd wait by the gate until the farmer came to pick him up. Jip also proved himself indispensable as a helper around the farm. He would frequently carry the farmer's lunch in a basket out to him as he worked in the field.

A large, dark mahogany Kelpie, Drummer was his master's constant companion. He

HEART-HEALTHY
In this modern age of ever-improving cardio-care, no doctor or scientist can dispute the advantages of owning a dog to lower a person's risk of heart disease. Studies have proven that petting a dog, walking a dog and grooming a dog all show positive results toward lowering your blood pressure. The simple routine of exercising your dog—going outside with the dog and walking, jogging or playing catch—is heart-healthy in and of itself. If you are normally less active than your physician thinks you should be, adopting a dog may be a smart option to improve your own quality of life as well as that of another creature.

loved to ride in the farmer's truck each day as they moved about the property. Once, when the farmer had to go away on business for two weeks, he left Drummer on the farm to guard the family and property. When the farmer returned, he stopped overnight at another one of his family's homes about 2 miles from the farm where Drummer was on watch. The next morning when he went out to his truck, Drummer was in the back of it, waiting to go to work with his boss. No one ever learned how

While the Kelpie is typically bored with the repetition of obedience training, he must learn the basic commands for his safety and good behavior.

the dog had known his master was back in town. Yet the dog had walked the miles from the farm to the town home and found his master's truck to take up his vigil.

These stories are just samples of Kelpie behavior that demonstrates their loyalty, intelligence and eagerness to please their owners. These stories and hundreds like them give solid testimony to the fact that Kelpies do not like to be separated from their masters. Consequently, they are not ideal pets for people who must leave their dogs at home for long hours each day while they go off to work. The Kelpie's devotion to master and family, combined with the breed's desire to work, makes him a poor candidate for suburban backyard pethood. However, Kelpies' mild dispositions and tractable intelligence, along with their inexhaustible energy, make them ideal dogs to work livestock and do chores around the farm.

Though breeders of working Kelpies prefer that their dogs be used for work, Kelpies have the potential to be successful in a number of dog sports. Of course the breed excels in herding events; breed clubs and multi-breed stockdog clubs offer these as ways to test and develop the Kelpie's innate skills. The sport of agility is another arena that

BOREDOM SPELLS TROUBLE

Kelpies without sufficient work to do can become so frustrated and bored that they begin to exhibit extremely undesirable behavior, such as chewing furniture, woodwork, clothing, etc. A bored Kelpie will bark incessantly for no apparent reason (actually, frustration is the reason) and will sometimes void in inappropriate places, such as in the house, on the porch, around the pool or on the owner's bed. Before long, the dog is so out of control that the owner decides he can't cope with the problem behavior anymore. He will then turn the dog over to an animal shelter. If the dog is lucky, he'll be rescued by someone who cares about the breed and is willing to put the Kelpie to work and help the dog develop a new and better lifestyle. If the dog is not lucky, he faces euthanasia. Therein lies the tragedy of the neglected pet dog or the mismatch between owner and breed.

offers exciting activity to Kelpies. Due to their athleticism, they quickly learn to master the art of jumping, climbing and making quick, sharp turns as they move from one obstacle to another. Running through long tunnel-like mazes is barely a challenge to these quick and agile dogs, and maneuvering across a see-saw becomes child's play once they learn how to do it.

Tracking, backpacking and scent-hurdle races are also attractive sports for Kelpies. In short, they adapt well to activities that offer fun, active participation and challenges to keep them mentally and physically stimulated. Heat, humidity, dry and dusty plains, flat deserts, rolling hills, mountainous terrain—the Kelpie adjusts to all types of climate and landscape. As long as he's with his master and keeping busy, he's happy.

The Kelpie's characteristics are fascinating elements of this unique breed of dog. Provided that the Kelpie owner recognizes and accepts the breed's natural traits and genetic tendencies, and especially if the owner puts his Kelpie to work, man and dog can enjoy many years of companionship and rewarding experiences together.

With typical herding body language, this Kelpie rounds up a wayward toy.

BREED STANDARD FOR THE

AUSTRALIAN KELPIE

A breed standard is a detailed word picture of what an ideal dog of that particular breed should look like. Usually a standard comes into existence when breeders and fanciers get together and form a breed club. That organization then proceeds to spell out the details of the desirable physical conformation, temperament and other important points of their breed. Eventually, the breed club applies to the national kennel club of their country for breed recognition and approval of the breed standard.

The breed standard for the Kelpie presents an interesting situation, as working Kelpies and show-type Kelpies have diverged much in type. The show-type Kelpies are seen in conformation shows whereas the working Kelpies are not; rather, the working-type dogs are judged according to their

While proponents of the Australian Kelpie do not stress strict adherence to the standard (as long as the dog's working ability is exemplified), dogs that are shown in conformation should measure up to the written ideal.

Coat color does not affect a dog's working ability, and the Kelpie standard allows for a range of striking colors and combinations.

performance in trials that evaluate their ability with livestock. Adherence to physical ideals is a secondary concern among breeders of the working-type Kelpie, with working ability and preservation of the breed's natural skills the foremost concern. Many working-type breeders feel that breeding with an eye to physical conformation is only to the detriment of the breed, believing that things like ears that don't stand erect or an unrecognized coat color have no bearing on a dog's capability as a stockdog. When physical traits are the main focus, desirable skills and temperament traits can be lost.

A standard for working-type Kelpies does exist in order to preserve general type in the breed and promote the physical characteristics necessary for the dog to do his intended work. However, it is stressed that the written description is a guideline only and that working ability must never be sacrificed in favor of beauty points. The following description is excerpted from that of the breed's homeland and used by the Working Kelpie Council of Australia. The full description, complete with further commentary on how these characteristics contribute to the dog's function and an explanation of undesirable traits, can be found at www.wkc.org.au. Readers interested in examining the differences in the two types of Kelpie should research the Fédération Cynologique Internationale's standard at www.fci.be, which is used by the Australian National Kennel Council (the country's main show-dog organization).

DESCRIPTION OF THE WORKING KELPIE

Characteristics: Extremely alert, eager and highly intelligent, with an open, friendly, active but placid disposition. Good balance between keenness to work and ability to relax. Almost inexhaustible energy; a marked loyalty and devotion to "work" and a strongly inherited natural instinct and aptitude in the working of sheep (and other livestock), both in open country and in the yards.

General Appearance: A medium sized, lithe, active, strongly muscled dog, possessing great suppleness of limb and conveying the capability of untiring work.

Movement: Gait should be free, smooth and effortless, with a good length of stride, showing a tendency for foot placement to move towards "single tracking" just before breaking into a trot and becoming more pronounced as speed increases. Ability to turn suddenly at speed, capable of the crouching stealthy movement demanded by its work. When walking slowly (and when standing still), the legs seen from front or rear should be four square.

Black and tan dog of pleasing balance, substance and structure in profile.

Prick ears and a
wedge shape
contribute to the
typical look of the
Kelpie's head.

Head: Slightly rounded skull, broad between well-pricked ears, forehead curved very slightly towards a pronounced stop. Cheeks neither coarse nor prominent but rounded to the foreface, cleanly chiseled and defined. Muzzle of moderate length, tapered toward the nose and refined in comparison to the skull. Lips tight and clean.

Teeth: Sound, strong and evenly spaced, the lower incisors just behind but touching the upper.

Eyes: Overall placement in the skull should provide the widest possible field of vision without the need of head movement. Slightly oval shaped, of medium size and widely spaced, clearly defined at the corners and showing a kind, intelligent and eager expression.

Ears: Widely spaced, pricked and running to a fine point at the tip, the leather fine but strong at the base, inclining outwards and slightly curved on the outer edge. Of moderate size. The inside of the ears well furnished with hair to discourage entry of foreign bodies.

Neck: Of fair length, strong, slightly arched and showing quality, gradually molding into the shoulders.

Forequarters: Clean, muscular, with sloping shoulders close-set at the withers; elbows set parallel with the body.

Shoulders: Clean, muscular, with a long sloping shoulder blade (scapula) set at approximately a 45° angle to the ground. Close-set withers, upper arm (humerus) forming a near 90° angle with the blade (scapula) and appropriately angulated to the forearm (radius and ulna) with elbows set parallel to the body. Particular emphasis should be placed on the sloping shoulder.

Forelegs: Clean, muscular, refined bone. Perfectly straight when viewed from the front. The length of leg should be approximately the same from the point of elbow (tip of the ulna) to the ground as is the distance from the withers to the base of the rib cage. Preference towards longer, rather than shorter, forelegs. The pastern should show a slight angle with the forearm when viewed from side.

Front Feet: Round, strong, deep in pad, with flexible well-arched toes. Strong short nails to allow the dog to adapt to differing ground surfaces.

Body: The chest should be deep, rather than wide; ribs well sprung (not barrel-ribbed) with a topline showing a rise at the withers (to allow sufficient action of the forequarters). Strong and well-muscled loins, sloping to the butt of the tail.

Length to Height Ratio: 10:9. The body, measured from the point of the breast bone in a straight line to the buttocks, should be greater than the height at the withers, as 10 units is to 9 units (e.g., a dog 18 inches in height should measure 20 inches in length).

Chest: When viewed from the side, should be deep, the point of breast bone showing ahead of the junction between shoulder blade (scapula) and upper arm (humerus). The bottom line of the rib cage should curve downwards from its point to below and slightly in front of the elbow (tip of the ulna), then remain level to the eighth rib before continuing in a gradual upwards curve towards the flank.

Hindquarters: Should show breadth and strength with the rump rather long and sloping. The upper thigh (femur) is well set into the hip socket at the pelvis at a corresponding angle to the shoulder blade. When viewed from the side, the overall upper line of the rump and tail should form a smooth curve when the dog is standing at rest. The stifles (junction of femur with tibia and fibula) are well turned (angled). The hocks are fairly well let down and placed parallel with the body when viewed from behind.

Hind Feet: Slightly elongated in comparison with the front feet. Strong, deep in the pads, with flexible well-arched toes. Strong, short nails to allow the dog maximum thrust under differing ground surfaces.

Tail: When viewed from the side the butt of the tail should be well let down. During inactivity, the tail should hang in a slight curve reaching the hock. Longer rather than shorter tail is desirable.

Size: Classified as a medium-sized dog. Height to length ratio of 9:10.

Coat: Moderately short, flat, straight and weather-resisting outer coat, with or without a short dense undercoat. Hair should be short on the head, ears, feet and legs. Coat can be slightly longer at the neck and rear of the thighs, and on the underside of the tail to form a brush.

Color: Any color and markings historically associated with the development of the breed. For example: black with or without tan; blue (gray) ranging from dark to light, with or without tan; red ranging from chocolate to light red, with or without tan; fawn ranging from dark to light, with or without tan; tan ranging from dark to cream. Tan markings range from dark tan to cream and are present in varying amounts.

UNDESIRABLE TRAITS IN PROFILE

Upright shoulders, flat-footed, too short-bodied, high on leg, lacking bone.

Low on leg, long back, short neck, knuckled over in front, soft topline.

Generally lacking substance, ewe-necked, weak pasterns, upright shoulders, lacking proper angle in the rear, ring tail.

Loaded upright shoulders, short neck, toeing out in front, high in the rear, cow-hocked, kinked tail.

This small puppy will grow into an intelligent and independent working dog. Are you ready for the challenges of Kelpie ownership?

AUSTRALIAN KELPIE

Before you begin your search for a puppy, you must research the Kelpie thoroughly and be sure that this is the most suitable breed for you, your family, your lifestyle and your living environment. While you must like the breed's characteristics, you must also be certain that you can provide for the breed's requirements. With the Kelpie, a major concern is that you can provide adequate space and time for the dog to exercise and play. This is a working breed and, although you may be keeping your Kelpie simply as a companion dog, you must always ensure that he has more than enough "work" to do in order for him to be happy, well-behaved and mentally sound.

In the case of the Kelpie, researching and reading up on the breed is not enough. Before deciding that this is the breed for you, breeders strongly recommend that you meet, observe and interact with some representatives of the breed. Visit a ranch or a stockdog trial to see these dogs in action and to get an idea of what they really are about. Once you see this intense working dog doing what he does best, you will understand why Kelpie breeders are not eager to sell to pet homes, and you will

also understand the true character of the breed. A potential owner who does not grasp the intensity of the Kelpie's drive to work will be very unhappy trying to live with one.

Puppies of any breed need lots of attention during the growing stage. They need to eat frequently and relieve themselves often. Furthermore, they chew on everything they can get their teeth into. Your puppy must be housebroken and taught good manners for a successful existence within the family group. He will bond easily with you, his new owners, to become a life partner with those who demonstrate concern for his happiness and well-being. As the dog matures, that bond helps create the dog's devotion to his family and regard for their safety.

A pet owner must be aware of the Kelpie's adolescent period, which usually starts around eight months of age and can last up to around two years of age. Kelpies are hard to live with in a pet setting during this time if the owners are not completely prepared to provide the Kelpie with the work, training, exercise and interaction that he requires.

Do you have time
to spend with your
Kelpie, doing
things together to
keep his body and
mind active?

This stage is not as problematic for the owner of a working Kelpie but can be overwhelming for the pet owner and often causes unprepared pet owners to give these dogs up for adoption at this age. Again, plenty of exercise and activity that uses the dog's body and brain is absolutely necessary at all stages of the Kelpie's life and even more so at this stage.

If you feel that you and the Kelpie are a good match but would prefer an adult dog, a mature dog is sometimes available for sale or adoption. Situations include death of an owner, a family that must move and cannot take the dog with them or a former brood bitch who is being retired from having puppies and must be placed in a private home as a family pet. Situations also arise in which pet owners simply were not prepared for the Kelpie's needs and are unable to keep the dog as a pet. These adult dogs can make fine companions, providing they have friendly, willing temperaments and are taken in by owners who understand the breed and can provide them with sufficient space and exercise.

With an adult dog, all of the developmental stages of growing up are over. The dog is usually housebroken and chewing stages are long gone. However, many Kelpies that are given up by pet owners are in their adolescent stage, during which the "go, go, go" mindset was too much for their previous owners to handle. And though bonding will take longer than with a puppy, the older dog can develop a strong relationship with new owners, providing he's treated with gentle kindness and patience.

THE FAMILY TREE
Your puppy's pedigree is his family tree. Just as a child may resemble his parents and grandparents, so too will a puppy reflect the qualities, good and bad, of his ancestors, especially those in the first two generations. Therefore it's important to know as much as possible about a puppy's immediate relatives. Reputable and experienced breeders should be able to explain the pedigree and why they chose to breed from the particular dogs they used.

Now, let's talk about the sex of your new dog. Females are usually more gentle and tend to stay closer to home than males. They can be very patient with young children and gentle with older adults. Males are usually more curious and tend to wander away from home more frequently. They also can be stronger-willed than females and frequently require a firmer leader. However, a stubborn, dominant female can be a real challenge, too.

As far as size, females are generally smaller than males. Size can vary quite a bit within the breed. While this is not a large breed, it is a very athletic and strong breed, with the strength of a much larger dog packed into a compact body.

In both cases, neutering the male and spaying the female is a must in order to get the most out of the relationship. Unless your pup has been deemed as having excellent potential for future breeding, spaying/neutering should be considered mandatory and may even be required in the breeder's sales contract. Left unaltered, dogs are controlled by their hormones. Their natural urges can be so strong and over-whelming that they never really develop strong bonds with their human pack members.

Males are governed by hormones full-time, 12 months a year. On the other hand, females are governed by hormones usually

FINDING A QUALIFIED BREEDER

Before you begin your puppy search, ask for references from your vet, other owners and other breeders to refer you to someone they believe is reputable. Responsible breeders usually raise only one or two breeds of dog. Avoid any breeder who has several different breeds or has several litters at the same time. Dedicated breeders are usually involved with a breed or other dog club. Many participate in some sport or activity related to their breed. Just as you want to be assured of the breeder's qualifications, the breeder wants to be assured that you will make a worthy owner. Expect the breeder to interview you, asking questions about your goals for the pup, your experience with dogs and what kind of home you will provide.

A litter of Kelpies means more than a little mischief!

twice a year for periods of 21 days at a time. This is the period known as estrus. A female in estrus will willingly accept any male dog that finds his way to her door during these heat cycles. As a result, the unaltered male frequently wanders the neighborhood in search of females in heat, and the female has unwanted puppies. Altering is the perfect solution to these situations. Altered dogs are generally nicer, more loving and more dedicated to home and family than sexually intact dogs.

Once you are sure that the Australian Kelpie is the breed for you, check with the Kelpie breed clubs and registries to get the names, addresses and phone numbers of Kelpie owners and breeders in your area. If you have a computer, the Internet can provide many references for Australian Kelpies; the breed club, Working Kelpies, Inc., is a good place to start. Talk to local

veterinarians to find out if they count Kelpies among their clients. Through these sources, you can meet Kelpie owners to see how they feel about the breed and if they have any recommendations for you as a prospective owner. Remember that the show-type Kelpies and working Kelpies differ considerably, so this will play a large role in your choice of a breeder. Talking to people within the breed can further acquaint you with the differences and can point you toward breeders of the type you prefer.

Most breeders of working Kelpies are insistent about their dogs' being used for work and will not sell to pet owners. If you are bringing a Kelpie into a pet home, your search for a breeder will be difficult. Finding a breeder

NEW RELEASES

Most breeders release their puppies between seven to ten weeks of age. A breeder who allows puppies to leave the litter at five or six weeks of age may be more concerned with profit than with the puppies' welfare. However, some breeders of show or working breeds may hold one or more top-quality puppies longer, occasionally until three or four months of age, in order to evaluate the puppies' career or show potential and decide which one(s) they will keep for themselves.

in your area will be even more difficult. Be wary of a Kelpie breeder who agrees to sell you a puppy without much thought to your living environment and your preparedness for the breed; this is not the type of breeder from whom you should purchase any breed.

Your efforts will be worth it when you find a reputable Kelpie breeder. Only the pup's breeder will know about the origin of the puppy, the background of the parents, any risk of hereditary health problems, how the puppy was raised, the pup's personality, etc. A good breeder will also offer help and support after the puppy comes home with you. Therefore, the best place to look for a Kelpie puppy is from a Kelpie breeder.

Your Kelpie puppy will not be an instant purchase. If you find a good breeder who agrees to sell you a puppy, you will likely be put on a waiting list for a suitable pup. If the breeder is far away,

Until properly trained, puppies must remain on lead when out and about.

you will not get to meet your puppy, and he will have to be shipped to you. Prior to that, you will contact the breeder by phone, email and/or mail; he should be able to share the important information with you in those ways, including pedigrees, photos of the litter and parents, puppy diet sheet, health records and documentation, etc.

A reputable Kelpie breeder devotes his energy and time to producing the best Kelpie puppies possible. He has studied the breed history, knows the health problems of the breed and has probably participated with his own breeding stock in events where knowledgeable judges have evaluated the quality of his dogs for future breeding purposes.

Most importantly, the breeder is anxious to share his knowledge of the breed with you. The breeder will probably ask you many questions about how you intend to raise his puppy and the facilities

SIGNS OF A HEALTHY PUPPY

Healthy puppies are robust little fellows who are alert and active, sporting shiny coats and supple skin. They should not appear lethargic, bloated or pot-bellied, nor should they have flaky skin or runny or crusted eyes or noses. Their stools should be firm and well formed, with no evidence of blood or mucus.

you have to provide a good, safe home for the puppy. In short, the Kelpie breeder is the best source of quality puppies and the best guide to help you find the puppy best suited to you, your family and your lifestyle. Be aware in your search for a pet puppy that you may be met with many "Nos" before you find a breeder who agrees to sell you a puppy.

Speaking of lifestyle, the breeder will need to know what type of lifestyle you will be offering the puppy. Will he grow up to be a herding dog on a 2000-acre sheep ranch? Will the dog work in a confined area, such as a stockyard, to move the flock from one area to another? Will he be a family pet and a companion to

Kelpies play as hard as they work and provide entertaining companionship for children and adults alike.

small children or elderly family members? Will the dog be expected to travel with his owner for business or pleasure? The more information you give the breeder, the better able he will be to decide if you have a suitable home for the breed.

How tragic it is for a puppy to go to an owner whose lifestyle is not suitable for the breed's temperament and the individual puppy's personality. And what a shame for an owner to discover that the puppy he wanted so much turned out to have the wrong personality for the family that chose him. By doing your homework now, you'll avoid all the pitfalls of random selection and lack of careful planning.

Instead, you and your new puppy will be well suited to each other.

Once you've located a respected breeder with a litter of puppies, make an appointment to visit them. This will be easier for those selecting a working dog, as there are many more breeders who place puppies in working homes. There will be lots of things you'll need to check out during your visit. First is the overall impression you get upon entering the breeder's home. Is it clean? Does it have a pleasant odor? Is the dam (the puppies' mother) there to meet you? Is she friendly and self-assured yet willing to meet you? What is her physical condition? After nursing a litter of puppies for five or six weeks, she may be thin, but she should have a clean coat and bright eyes and appear to be in good health.

Be aware that the mother's

basic temperament will be passed on to her pups, so spend a few minutes with her and observe her reactions to you, the breeder and her pups. An unfriendly, aloof, even aggressive mother will probably raise pups with the same undesirable traits. So look for a friendly, tolerant, easygoing dam who accepts you cautiously yet willingly.

Healthy puppies are active, alert and playful.

Initially observe the whole litter as they interact with each other and you. If possible, watch them eat a meal. If you spot a particular pup who appears to be overprotective of his food, that puppy may become a problem in the future. You don't need trouble with an adult dog who is so protective of his food and toys that he threatens to bite you every time you get near him when he's eating or playing.

Do the puppies appear healthy and bright-eyed, with no discharge from their eyes or noses? Are they clean? Do they

GETTING ACQUAINTED

When visiting a litter, ask the breeder for suggestions on how best to interact with the puppies. If possible, get right into the middle of the pack and sit down with them. Observe which pups climb into your lap and which ones shy away. Toss a toy for them to chase and bring back to you. It's easy to fall in love with the puppy who picks you, but keep your future objectives in mind before you make your final decision.

smell clean when you pick them up? When they have bowel movements, are their stools firm and well-formed with no hint of diarrhea? Are their coats fluffy and free of parasites and foreign matter such as grass, twigs, leaves, etc.?

As you begin to focus on

SELECTING FROM THE LITTER
Before you visit a litter of puppies, promise yourself that you won't fall for the first adorable face you see! Decide on your goals for your puppy—herding dog, show prospect, competitor, family companion—and then look for a puppy who displays the appropriate qualities. In most litters, there is an alpha pup (the bossy puppy), and occasionally a shy fellow who is less confident, with the rest of the litter falling somewhere in the middle. "Middle-of-the-roaders" are safe bets for most families.

particular puppies in the litter, concentrate on studying their behavior, as it usually predicts what they'll be like as adults. For example, the bully in a litter may turn out to be a very dominant individual who is difficult to control. The smallest one may grow up to be very timid or, conversely, extremely tyrannical, challenging every other dog he meets.

A friendly, outgoing, yet not hyperactive, puppy begins life with a lot in his favor. He will be easy to train, work with and live with. His curiosity and alertness indicates his potential intelligence, and raising him will be fun, interesting and rewarding.

One final note: look for the puppy that, by his behavior, indicates that he wants to be with people rather than with his littermates. Some dogs are "dog dogs" and some are "people dogs." "Dog dogs" are happiest when they're with their own kind, while "people dogs" find pleasure in human company and are, therefore, easiest to raise and live with.

At some point during your visit, the breeder may mention that he considers one or more of the puppies to be of breeding or show quality. While the focus in the Kelpie breed is on preserving working ability rather than producing show dogs, the breed standard is still a valuable tool.

There are those who show their Kelpies in conformation shows. When planning a specific mating, the reputable breeder strives to produce puppies that will grow up to represent the breed as best as possible in the stockyard or the show ring, depending on the breeder. If a puppy develops into a top-quality specimen, the pup must be kept sexually intact. The working-type breeder wants to get this puppy into a home where his working instincts will be utilized; the show-type Kelpie breeder wants the pup to be shown in conformation. These are the dogs that are used for breeding and contribute to future generations of the breed.

Finally, you'll want to ask the breeder about pedigrees, kennel club registration papers and health records and certificates. A pedigree is a genealogical record of the puppies' forebears. It will also tell you who of the puppy's ancestors among the past four generations earned titles in performance events or shows. There are many titles available for dogs to earn, and you may be interested in getting involved in competitions with your Kelpie as he matures. If you are interested in a particular area of competition, look for a pup whose ancestors were achievers in that area. By knowing about the accomplishments of your puppy's parents and grandparents, you can better

> ## PUPPY PARASITES
> Parasites are nasty little critters that live in or on your dog or puppy. Most puppies are born with ascarid roundworms, which are acquired from dormant ascarids residing in the dam. Other parasites can be acquired through contact with infected fecal matter. Take a stool sample to your vet for testing. He will prescribe a safe wormer to treat any parasites found in your puppy's stool. Always have a fecal test performed at your puppy's annual veterinary exam.

appreciate your dog's future potential.

You are entitled to registration papers from a national registry, which the breeder will provide. These papers give the names and registration numbers of the puppy's parents, the name of the breeder, the date and place of the pup's birth and the litter number from which the pup came. The breeder should also supply you

A Kelpie in his element. Learn all you can about your puppy's lineage and the depth of working ability over several generations.

with an individual certificate of application, which you must fill out and submit to register your own dog. That application also requires you to submit the name you have chosen for your new puppy.

A health certificate from a veterinarian should also accompany the puppy when you purchase him. That certificate should list any immunizations given to the puppy by the veterinarian as well as any future shots that will be required.

Various breeds of dog have various hereditary and other health problems particular to their breed. Australian Kelpie owners, however, are blessed to have one of the healthiest breeds of all. There are, however, some problems that need to be mentioned. In Australian Kelpies, genetic bone disorders have been found as well as progressive retinal atrophy (PRA), a degenerative eye disease that eventually

leads to blindness. Hip dysplasia is occasionally found in Kelpies; this is a problem that has been seen in many breeds of dog. It is the malformation of the hip's ball-and-socket joint. In some dogs, the problem is severe and causes pain and lameness. In other cases, the problem is mild, and the dog can live his entire life without suffering or showing signs of discomfort. In the case of elbow dysplasia, a similar problem, the ulna (a bone in the upper arm) fails to fuse with the rest of the bone of the arm, resulting in abnormal development that causes lameness and pain.

Both of these conditions can be detected by testing once the dog is two years old. A certifying organization such as the Orthopedic Foundation for Animals (OFA) will issue the results of the tests and give certification to those dogs deemed suitable for breeding. Ask the breeder to see certification on both of your pup's parents, as reputable breeders only breed from certified dysplasia-free animals.

The Canine Eye Registration Foundation (CERF) issues similar clearances for dogs found to be free of eye diseases such as progressive retinal atrophy and cataracts, both of which cause blindness. Reputable breeders are anxious to identify and eliminate dogs from their breed's gene pool

THE FIRST FAMILY MEETING

Your puppy's first day at home should be quiet and uneventful. Despite his wagging tail, he is still wondering where his mom and siblings are! Let him make friends with other members of the family on his own terms; don't overwhelm him. You have a lifetime ahead to get to know each other!

Among the herding breeds, Kelpies are known for their affinity for children.

who carry hereditary health problems. This is one more reason why purchasing a pet from a responsible breeder greatly increases the odds of a healthy and sound puppy.

YOUR AUSTRALIAN KELPIE SHOPPING LIST

Just as expectant parents prepare a nursery for their baby, so should you ready your home for the arrival of your Australian Kelpie pup. If you have the necessary puppy supplies purchased and in place before he comes home, it will ease the puppy's transition from the warmth and familiarity of his mom and littermates to the brand-new environment of his new home and human family. You will be too busy to stock up and prepare your house after your pup comes home, that's for sure! Imagine how a pup must feel upon being transported to a strange new place. It's up to you to comfort him and to let your little pup know that he is going to be happy with you!

FOOD AND WATER BOWLS

Your puppy will need separate bowls for his food and water. Stainless steel pans are generally preferred over plastic bowls since

Stainless steel bowls are popular choices as they are durable, easy to clean and resistant to chewing.

they sterilize better and pups are less inclined to chew on the metal. Heavy-duty ceramic bowls are popular, but consider how often you will have to pick up those heavy bowls. Buy adult-sized pans, as your puppy will grow into them quickly.

THE DOG CRATE

If you think that crates are tools of punishment and confinement for when a dog has misbehaved, think again. Most breeders and almost all trainers recommend a crate as the preferred house-training aid as well as for all-around puppy training and safety. Because dogs are natural den creatures that prefer cave-like environments, the benefits of crate use are many. The crate provides the puppy with his very own "safe house," a cozy place to sleep, take a break or seek comfort with a favorite toy; a travel aid to house your dog when on the road, at motels or at the vet's office; a training aid to help teach your puppy proper toileting habits; and a place of solitude when non-dog people happen to

Crates can be purchased at your local pet-supply shop. Since the crate should last a dog's lifetime, get one large enough for a fully grown dog.

drop by and don't want a lively puppy—or even a well-behaved adult dog—saying hello or begging for attention.

Crates come in several types, although the wire crate and the fiberglass airline-type crate are the most popular. Both are safe and your puppy will adjust to either one, so the choice is up to you. The wire crates offer better visibility for the pup as well as better ventilation. Many of the wire crates easily collapse into suitcase-size carriers. The fiberglass crates, similar to those used by the airlines for animal transport, are sturdier and more den-like. However, the fiberglass crates do not collapse and are less ventilated than wire crates; this can be problematic in hot weather. Some of the newer crates are made of heavy plastic mesh; they are very lightweight and fold up into

slim-line suitcases. However, a mesh crate might not be suitable for a pup with manic chewing habits.

Don't bother with a puppy-sized crate. Although your Australian Kelpie will be a little fellow when you bring him home, he will grow up in the blink of an eye and your puppy crate will be useless. Purchase a crate that will accommodate an adult Australian Kelpie. The Kelpie is a medium-sized dog, but size can vary, so use the breeder's knowledge of how his line matures to help you predict your Kelpie's eventual size.

BEDDING AND CRATE PADS

Your puppy will enjoy some type of soft bedding in his "room" (the crate), something he can snuggle into to feel cozy and secure. Old towels or blankets are good choices for a young pup, since he may (and probably will) have a toileting accident or two in the crate or decide to chew on the bedding material. Once he is fully trained and out of the early chewing stage, you can replace the puppy bedding with a permanent crate pad if you prefer. Crate pads and other dog beds run the gamut from inexpensive to high-end doggie-designer styles, but don't splurge on the good stuff until you are sure that your puppy is reliable and won't tear it up or make a mess on it.

PUPPY TOYS

Just as infants and older children require objects to stimulate their minds and bodies, puppies need toys to entertain their curious brains, wiggly paws and achy teeth. A fun array of safe doggie toys will help satisfy your puppy's chewing instincts and distract him from gnawing on the leg of your antique chair or your

One of the first things a pup will do when released from his crate is sniff around for a pleasing potty spot.

Feeding your Kelpie in his crate a few times in the beginning will help him associate the crate with good things.

A crate is helpful for confining a dog safely during travel. This dog's owners have gone a step further with a custom dog trailer.

new leather sofa. Most puppy toys are cute and look as if they would be a lot of fun, but not all are necessarily safe or good for your puppy, so use caution when you go puppy-toy shopping.

Australian Kelpies can be chewers, especially when bored, so be prepared with plenty of sturdy toys. The best "chewci-fiers" are nylon and hard rubber bones, which are safe to gnaw on and come in sizes appropriate for all age groups and breeds. Be especially careful of natural bones, which can splinter or develop dangerous sharp edges; pups can easily swallow or choke on those bone splinters. Veterinarians often tell of surgical nightmares involving bits of splintered bone, because in addition to the danger of choking,

the sharp pieces can damage the intestinal tract.

Similarly, rawhide chews, while a favorite of most dogs and puppies, can be equally dangerous. Pieces of rawhide are easily swallowed after they get soft and gummy from chewing, and dogs have been known to choke on pieces of ingested rawhide. Rawhide chews should be offered only when you can supervise the puppy.

Soft woolly toys are special puppy favorites. They come in a wide variety of cute shapes and sizes; some look like little stuffed animals. Puppies love to shake them up and toss them about or simply carry them around, but they don't often last long. Be careful of fuzzy toys that have button eyes or noses that your pup could chew off and swallow, and make sure that he does not disembowel a squeaky toy to remove the squeaker. Braided rope toys are similar in that they are fun to chew and toss around, but they shred easily and the strings are easy to swallow. The strings are not digestible and, if the puppy doesn't pass them in his stool, he could end up at the vet's office. As with rawhides, your puppy should be closely monitored with rope toys.

If you believe that your pup has ingested a piece of one of his toys, check his stools for the next couple of days to see if he passes them when he defecates. At the same time, also watch for signs of intestinal distress. A call to your veterinarian might be in order to get his advice and be on the safe side.

An all-time favorite toy for puppies (young and old!) is the

TOYS 'R SAFE

The vast array of tantalizing puppy toys is staggering. Stroll through any pet shop or pet-supply outlet and you will see that the choices can be overwhelming. However, not all dog toys are safe or sensible. Most very young puppies enjoy soft woolly toys that they can snuggle with and carry around. (You know they have outgrown them when they shred them up!) Avoid toys that have buttons, tabs or other enhancements that can be chewed off and swallowed. Soft toys that squeak are fun, but make sure your puppy does not disembowel the toy and remove (and swallow) the squeaker. Toys that rattle or make noise can excite a puppy, but they present the same danger as the squeaky kind and so require supervision. Hard rubber toys that bounce can also entertain a pup, but make sure that the toy is too big for your pup to swallow.

Engage your Kelpie in interactive games with his toys and his favorite playmate—you!

empty gallon milk jug. Hard plastic juice containers—46 ounces or more—are also excellent. Such containers make lots of noise when they are batted about, and puppies go crazy with delight as they play with them. However, they don't often last very long, so be sure to remove and replace them when they get chewed up.

Jumping up and making the catch. The Kelpie is a naturally athletic breed that can excel in sports and activities for competition or just for fun.

A word of caution about homemade toys: be careful with your choices of non-traditional play objects. Never use old shoes or socks, since a puppy cannot distinguish between the old ones on which he's allowed to chew and the new ones in your closet that are strictly off limits. That principle applies to anything that resembles something that you don't want your puppy to chew.

COLLARS

A lightweight nylon collar is the best choice for a very young pup. Quick-click collars are easy to put

COLLARING OUR CANINES

The standard flat collar with a buckle or a snap, in leather, nylon or cotton, is widely regarded as the everyday all-purpose collar. If the collar fits correctly, you should be able to fit two fingers between the collar and the dog's neck.

Leather Buckle Collars

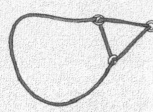

Limited-Slip Collar

The martingale, Greyhound or limited-slip collar is preferred by many dog owners and trainers. It is fixed with an extra loop that tightens when pressure is applied to the leash. The martingale collar gets tighter but does not "choke" the dog. The limited-slip collar should only be used for walking and training, not for free play or interaction with another dog. These types of collar should never be left on the dog, as the extra loop can lead to accidents.

Choke collars, usually made of stainless steel, are made for training purposes but are not recommended for certain breeds. The chains can injure small dogs or damage long/abundant coats and are also considered inappropriate for some breeds or individual dogs. Thin nylon choke leads are commonly used on show dogs while in the ring, though they are not practical for everyday use.

Snap-Bolt Choke Collar

The harness, with two or three straps that attach over the dog's shoulders and around his torso, is a humane and safe alternative to the conventional collar. By and large, a well-made harness is virtually escape-proof. Harnesses are available in nylon and mesh and can be outfitted on most dogs, with chest girths ranging from 10 to 30 inches.

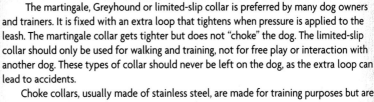

Harness

Nylon Collar

Quick-Click Closure

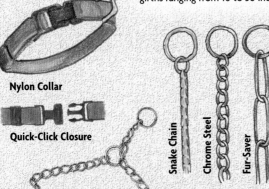

Snake Chain

Chrome Steel

Fur-Saver

Choke Chain Collars

A head collar, composed of a nylon strap that goes around the dog's muzzle and a second strap that wraps around his neck, offers the owner better control over his dog. This device is recommended for problem-solving with dogs (including jumping up, pulling and aggressive behaviors) but must be used with care.

A training halter, including a flat collar and two straps, made of nylon and webbing, is designed for walking. There are several on the market; some are more difficult to put on the dog than others. The halter harness, with two small slip rings at each end, is recommended for ease of use.

Leash Life

Dogs love leashes! Believe it or not, most dogs dance for joy every time their owners pick up their leashes. The leash means that the dog is going for a walk—and there are few things more exciting than that! Here are some of the kinds of leashes that are commercially available.

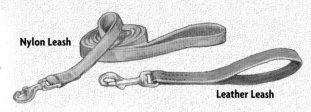

Nylon Leash

Leather Leash

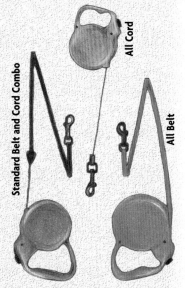

Standard Belt and Cord Combo

All Cord

All Belt

Retractable Leashes

Traditional Leash: Made of cotton, nylon or leather, these leashes are usually about 6 feet in length. A quality-made leather leash is softer on the hands than a nylon one. Durable woven cotton is a popular option. Lengths can vary up to about 48 feet, designed for different uses.

Chain Leash: Usually a metal chain leash with a plastic handle. This is not the best choice for most breeds, as it is heavier than other leashes and difficult to manage.

Retractable Leash: A long nylon cord is housed in a plastic device for extending and retracting. This type of leash is ideal for taking trained dogs for long walks in open areas, although it is not always suitable for large, powerful breeds. Different lengths and sizes are available, so check that you purchase one appropriate for your dog's weight.

Elastic Leash: A nylon leash with an elastic extension. This is useful for well-trained dogs, especially in conjunction with a head halter. Avoid leashes that are completely elastic, as they afford minimal control to the handler.

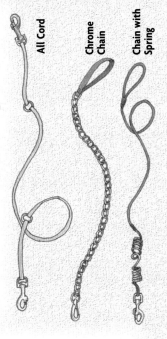

All Cord

Chrome Chain

Chain with Spring

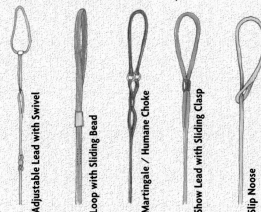

Adjustable Lead with Swivel

Loop with Sliding Bead

Martingale / Humane Choke

Show Lead with Sliding Clasp

Slip Noose

A Variety of Collar-and-Leash-in-One Products

Adjustable Leash: This has two snaps, one on each end, and several metal rings. It is handy if you need to tether your dog temporarily, but is never to be used with a choke collar.

Tab Leash: A short leash (4 to 6 inches long) that attaches to your dog's collar. This device serves like a handle, in case you have to grab your dog while he's exercising off lead. It's ideal for "half-trained" dogs or dogs that listen only half of the time.

Slip Leash: Essentially a leash with a collar built in, similar to what a dog-show handler uses to show a dog. This British-style collar has a ring on the end so that you can form a slip collar. Useful if you have to catch your own runaway dog or a stray.

on and remove, and they can be adjusted as the puppy grows. Introduce him to his collar as soon as he comes home to get him accustomed to wearing it. He'll get used to it quickly and won't mind a bit. Make sure that it is snug enough that it won't slip off, yet loose enough to be comfortable for the pup. You should be able to slip two fingers between the collar and his neck. Check the collar often, as puppies grow in spurts, and his collar can become too tight almost overnight.

LEASHES

A 6-foot nylon lead is an excellent choice for a young puppy. It is lightweight and not as tempting to chew as a leather lead. You can switch to a 6-foot leather lead after your pup has grown and is used to walking politely on a lead. For initial puppy walks and house-training purposes, you should invest in a shorter lead so that you have more control over the puppy. At first, you don't want him wandering too far away from you, and when taking him out for toileting you will want to keep him in the specific area chosen for his potty spot.

Once the puppy is heel trained with a traditional leash, you can consider purchasing a retractable lead. A retractable lead is good for walking adult dogs that

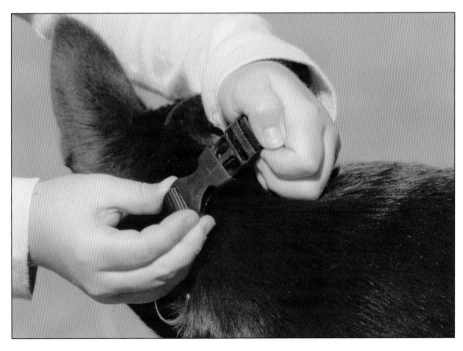

A quick-click collar is a wise choice for a puppy, as they can easily be put on and taken off.

For a dedicated
and knowledge-
able family, two
Kelpies bring
double the joy.

are already leash-wise. This type of lead lengthens to allow the dog to roam farther away from you and explore a wider area when out walking, and also retracts when you need to keep him close to you.

HOME SAFETY FOR YOUR PUPPY

The importance of puppy-proofing cannot be overstated. In addition to making your house comfortable for your Australian Kelpie's arrival, you also must make sure that your house is safe for your puppy before you bring him home. There are countless hazards in the owner's personal living environment that a pup can sniff, chew, swallow or destroy. Many are obvious; others are not. Do a thorough advance house check to remove or rearrange those things that could hurt your puppy, keeping any potentially dangerous items out of areas to which he will have access.

Electrical cords are especially dangerous, since puppies view them as irresistible chew toys. Unplug and remove all exposed cords or fasten them beneath baseboards where the puppy cannot reach them. Veterinarians and firefighters can tell you horror stories about electrical burns and house fires that resulted from puppy-chewed electrical cords. Consider this a most serious precaution for your puppy and the rest of your family.

Scout your home for tiny objects that might be seen at a pup's eye level. Keep medication bottles and cleaning supplies well out of reach, and do the same with waste baskets and other trash containers. It goes without saying that you should not use rodent poison or other toxic chemicals in any puppy area and that you must keep such containers safely locked up. You will be amazed at how many places a curious puppy can discover!

Once your house has cleared inspection, check your yard. A sturdy fence, well embedded into the ground, will give your dog a safe place to play and potty. Kelpies are curious and athletic dogs, so a 6-foot-high fence is the minimum requirement to contain an agile youngster or adult. Check the fence periodically for necessary repairs. If there is a weak link or space to squeeze through, you can be sure a determined Australian Kelpie will discover it.

The garage and shed can be hazardous places for a pup, as things like fertilizers, chemicals and tools are usually kept there. It's best to keep these areas off limits to the pup. Antifreeze is especially dangerous to dogs, as they find the taste appealing and it takes only a few licks from the

Don't let your snooping Kelpie stick his nose into trouble!

A Dog-Safe Home

The dog-safety police are taking you on a house tour. Let's go room by room and see how safe your own home is for your new Kelpie. The following items are doggy dangers, so either they must be removed or the dog should be monitored or not allowed access to these areas.

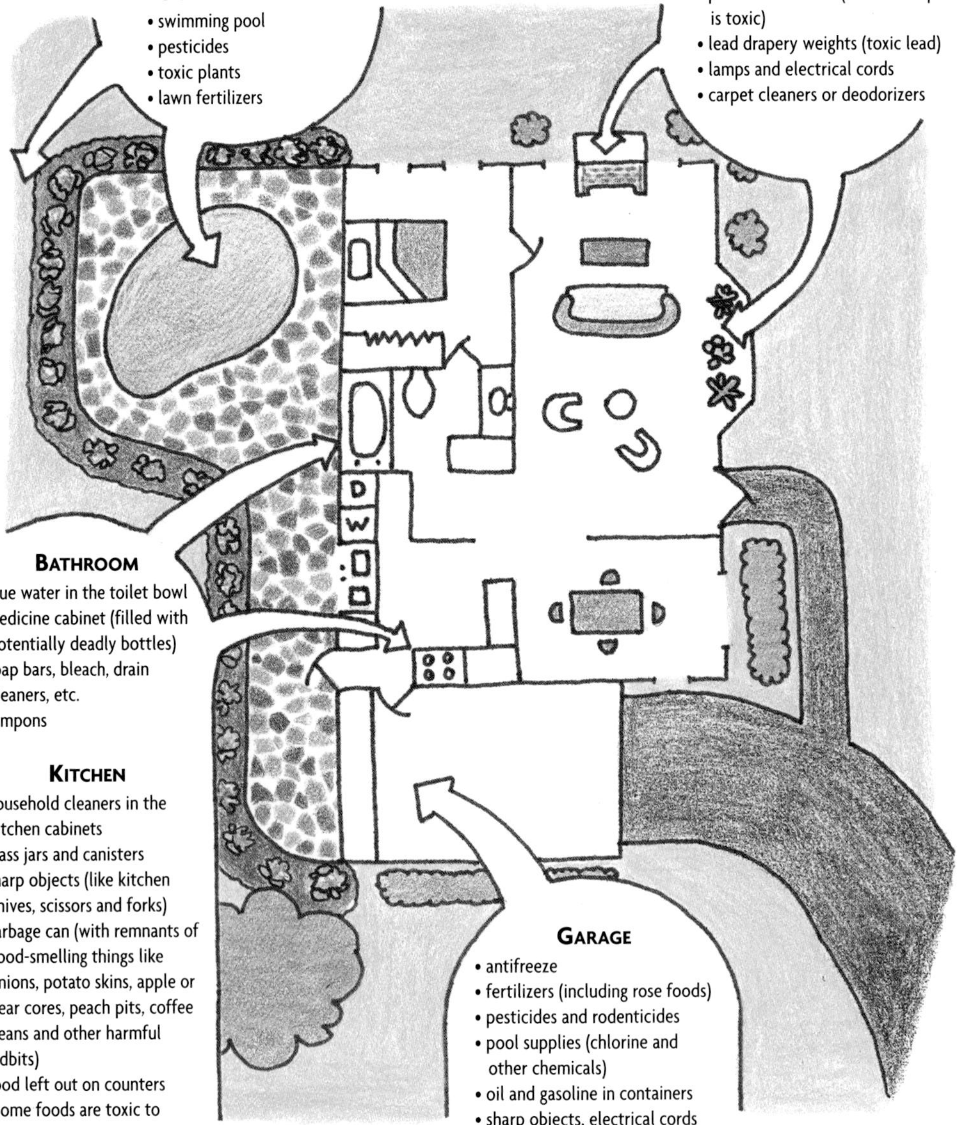

Living Room

- house plants (some varieties are poisonous)
- fireplace or wood-burning stove
- paint on the walls (lead-based paint is toxic)
- lead drapery weights (toxic lead)
- lamps and electrical cords
- carpet cleaners or deodorizers

Outdoors

- swimming pool
- pesticides
- toxic plants
- lawn fertilizers

Bathroom

- blue water in the toilet bowl
- medicine cabinet (filled with potentially deadly bottles)
- soap bars, bleach, drain cleaners, etc.
- tampons

Kitchen

- household cleaners in the kitchen cabinets
- glass jars and canisters
- sharp objects (like kitchen knives, scissors and forks)
- garbage can (with remnants of good-smelling things like onions, potato skins, apple or pear cores, peach pits, coffee beans and other harmful tidbits)
- food left out on counters (some foods are toxic to dogs)

Garage

- antifreeze
- fertilizers (including rose foods)
- pesticides and rodenticides
- pool supplies (chlorine and other chemicals)
- oil and gasoline in containers
- sharp objects, electrical cords and power tools

driveway to kill a dog, puppy or adult, small breed or large.

VISITING THE VETERINARIAN

A good veterinarian is your Australian Kelpie puppy's best health-insurance policy. If you do not already have a vet, ask your breeder, friends and experienced dog people for recommendations in your area so that you can select a vet before you bring your Australian Kelpie puppy home. Also arrange for your puppy's first veterinary examination beforehand, since many vets have waiting periods and your puppy should visit the vet within a day or so of coming home.

It's important to make sure your puppy's first visit to the vet is a pleasant and positive one. The vet should take great care to befriend the pup and handle him gently to make their first meeting a positive experience. The vet will give the pup a thorough physical examination and set up a schedule for vaccinations and other necessary wellness visits. Be sure to show your vet any health and inoculation records, which you should have received from your breeder. Your vet is a great source of canine health information, so be sure to ask questions and take notes. Creating a health journal for your puppy will make a handy reference for his wellness and any future health problems that may arise.

The Kelpie loves life on the farm with plenty of work for him to do.

OUTDOOR DANGERS
Plants are natural puppy magnets, but many can be harmful, even fatal, if ingested by a puppy or adult dog. Scout your yard and home interior and remove any plants, bushes or flowers that could be even mildly dangerous. It could save your puppy's life. You can obtain a complete list of toxic plants from your veterinarian, at the public library or by looking online. Grass that has been chemically treated also poses a danger, so be careful about where your Kelpie exercise.

MEETING THE FAMILY

Your Australian Kelpie's homecoming is an exciting time for all members of the family, and it's only natural that everyone will be eager to meet him, pet him and play with him. However, for the puppy's sake, it's best to make these initial family meetings as uneventful as possible so that the pup is not overwhelmed with too much too soon. Remember, he has just left his dam and his littermates and is away from the breeder's home for the first time. Despite his fuzzy wagging tail, he is still apprehensive and wondering where he is and who all these strange humans are. It's best to let him explore on his own and meet the family members as he feels comfortable. Let him investigate all the new smells, sights and sounds at his own pace. Children should be especially careful to not get overly excited, use loud voices or hug the pup too tightly. Be calm, gentle and affectionate, and be ready to comfort him if he appears frightened or uneasy.

Be sure to show your puppy his new crate during this first day home. Toss a treat or two inside the crate; if he associates the crate with food, he will associate the crate with good things. If he is comfortable with the crate, you can offer him his first meal inside it. Leave the door ajar so he can wander in and out as he chooses.

FIRST NIGHT IN HIS NEW HOME

So much has happened in your Kelpie puppy's first day away from the breeder. He's had his first car ride to his new home. He's met his new human family and perhaps the other family pets. He has explored his new house and yard, at least those places where he is to be allowed during his first weeks at home. He may have visited his new veterinarian. He has eaten his first meal or two away from his dam and litter-mates. Surely that's enough to tire out an eight-week-old Australian Kelpie pup—or so you hope!

It's bedtime. During the day, the pup investigated his crate, which is his new den and sleeping space, so it is not entirely strange to him. Line the crate with a soft towel or blanket that he can snuggle into and gently place him into the crate for the night. Some breeders send home a piece of bedding from where the pup slept with his littermates, and those familiar scents are a great comfort for the puppy on his first night without his siblings.

He will probably whine or cry. The puppy is objecting to the confinement and the fact that he is alone for the first time. This can be a stressful time for you as well as for the pup. It's important that you remain strong and don't let the puppy out of his crate to comfort him. He will fall asleep eventually. If you release him, the puppy will learn that crying means "out" and will continue that habit. You are laying the groundwork for future habits. Some breeders find that soft music can soothe a crying pup and help him get to sleep.

SOCIALIZING YOUR PUPPY

The first 16 weeks of your Australian Kelpie puppy's life are

KEEP OUT OF REACH

Most dogs don't browse around your medicine cabinet, but accidents do happen! The drug acetaminophen, the active ingredient in certain popular over-the-counter pain relievers, can be deadly to dogs and cats if ingested in large quantities. Acetaminophen toxicity, caused by the dog's swallowing 15 to 20 tablets, can be manifested in abdominal pains within a day or two of ingestion, as well as liver damage. If you suspect your dog has swiped a bottle of medication, get the dog to the vet immediately so that the vet can induce vomiting and cleanse the dog's stomach.

the most important of his entire lifetime. A properly socialized puppy will grow up to be a confident and stable adult who will be a pleasure to live with and a welcome addition to the neighborhood.

The importance of socialization cannot be overemphasized. Research on canine behavior has proven that puppies who are not exposed to new sights, sounds,

Some Kelpies dive headfirst into investigating an interesting scent.

people and animals during their first 16 weeks of life, the socialization period, will grow up to be timid and fearful, even aggressive, and unable to flourish outside of their home environment.

Socializing your puppy is not difficult and, in fact, will be a fun time for you both. Lead training goes hand in hand with socialization, so your puppy will be learning how to walk on a lead at the same time that he's meeting the neighborhood. Because the Australian Kelpie is a such an interesting breed, your neighbors will enjoy meeting "the new kid on the block." Take him for short walks to the park and to other dog-friendly places where he will encounter new people, especially children. Puppies automatically recognize children as "little

SOCIALIZATION STAGE
There is a window of opportunity in the lives of puppies that lasts for a brief eight weeks. Between the ages of 8 weeks and 16 weeks, a puppy is in the socialization stage of development. During those weeks, a puppy needs to get out among other people and other pets and learn that all of them are friendly and non-threatening. It's also at this time that a puppy needs to begin learning his basic manners and how to inhibit his chewing and biting reflexes so he can live peacefully with others for the rest of his life. The rancher may want to retain his pup's nipping instincts for working purposes but discourage him from "herding" up the family members in this manner.

When it comes to playtime, the Kelpie's always game!

people" and are drawn to play with them. Just make sure that you supervise these meetings and that the children do not get too rough or encourage him to play too hard. An overzealous pup can often nip too hard, frightening the child and in turn making the puppy overly excited. A bad experience in puppyhood can impact a dog for life, so a pup that has a negative experience with a child may grow up to be shy or even aggressive around children.

Take your puppy along on your daily errands. Puppies are natural "people magnets," and most people who see your pup will want to pet him. All of these encounters will help to mold him into a confident adult dog. Likewise, you will soon feel like a confident, responsible dog owner, rightly proud of your mannerly Australian Kelpie.

Be especially careful of your puppy's encounters and experiences during the eight-to-ten-week-old period, which is also called the "fear period." This is a serious imprinting period, and all contact during this time should be gentle and positive. A frightening or negative event could leave a permanent impression that could affect his future behavior if a similar situation arises.

Also make sure that your puppy has received his first and second rounds of vaccinations before you expose him to other dogs or bring him to places that other dogs may frequent. Avoid dog parks and other strange-dog

areas until your vet assures you that your puppy is fully immunized and resistant to the diseases that can be passed between canines. Discuss safe early socialization with your breeder and vet, as some recommend socializing the puppy even before he has received all of his inoculations.

Even the hard-working Kelpie can find time for some attention.

CREATE A SCHEDULE

Puppies thrive on sameness and routine. Offer meals at the same time each day, take him out at regular times for potty trips and do the same for play periods and outdoor activity. Make note of when your puppy naps and when he is most lively and energetic, and try to plan his day around those times. Once he is house-trained and more predictable in his habits, he will be better able to tolerate changes in his schedule.

LEADER OF THE PUPPY'S PACK

Like other canines, your puppy needs an authority figure, someone he can look up to and regard as the leader of his "pack." His first pack leader was his dam, who taught him to be polite and not chew too hard on her ears or nip at her muzzle. He learned those same lessons from his litter-mates. If he played too rough, they cried in pain and stopped the game, which sent an important message to the rowdy puppy.

The Kelpie forms a special bond with his entire family, serving as friend, helper and protector to young and old.

The Kelpie forms a special bond with his entire family, serving as friend, helper and protector to young and old.

As puppies play together, they are also struggling to determine who will be the boss. Being pack animals, dogs need someone to be in charge. If a litter of puppies remained together beyond puppyhood, one of the pups would emerge as the strongest one, the one who calls the shots.

Once your puppy leaves the pack, he will look intuitively for a new leader. If he does not recognize you as that leader, he will try to assume that position for himself. Of course, it is hard to imagine your adorable Kelpie puppy trying to be in charge when he is so small and seemingly helpless. You must remember that these are natural canine instincts. Do not cave in and allow your pup to get the upper "paw"!

Just as socialization is so important during these first 16 weeks, so too is your puppy's early education. He was born without any bad habits. He does not know what is good or bad behavior. If he does things like nipping and digging, it's because he is having fun and doesn't know that humans consider these things as "bad." It's your job to teach him proper puppy manners, and this is the best time to accomplish that—before he has developed bad habits, since it is much more difficult to "unlearn" or correct unacceptable learned behavior than to teach good behavior from the start.

Make sure that all members of the family understand the importance of being consistent when training their new puppy. If you tell the puppy to stay off the sofa and your daughter allows him to cuddle on the couch to watch her favorite television show, your pup will be confused about what he is and is not allowed to do. Have a family conference before your pup comes home so that everyone understands the basic principles

WATCH THE WATER
To help your puppy sleep through the night without having to relieve himself, remove his water bowl after 7 P.M. Offer him a couple of ice cubes during the evening to quench his thirst. Never leave water in a puppy's crate, as this is inviting puddles of mishaps.

of puppy training and the rules you have set forth for the pup, and agrees to follow them.

The old saying that "an ounce of prevention is worth a pound of cure" is especially true when it comes to puppies. It is much easier to prevent inappropriate behavior than it is to change it. It's also easier and less stressful for the pup, since it will keep discipline to a minimum and create a more positive learning environment for him. That, in turn, will also be easier on you!

Here are a few commonsense tips to keep your belongings safe and your puppy out of trouble:

- Keep your closet doors closed and your shoes, socks and other apparel off the floor so your puppy can't get to them.
- Keep a secure lid on the trash container or put the trash where your puppy can't dig into it. He can't damage what he can't reach!
- Supervise your puppy at all times to make sure he is not getting into mischief. If he starts to chew the corner of the rug, you can distract him instantly by tossing a toy for him to fetch. You also will be able to whisk him outside when you notice that he is about to piddle on the carpet. If you can't see your puppy, you can't teach him or correct his behavior.

SOLVING PUPPY PROBLEMS

CHEWING AND NIPPING

Nipping at fingers and toes is normal puppy behavior; with a herding dog, nipping at heels is also quite common. This is a way that they get their charges moving, which can be extended to people or other animals. Chewing is also the way that puppies investigate their surroundings. However, you will have to teach your puppy that chewing anything other than his toys is not acceptable. That won't happen overnight and at times puppy teeth will test your patience. However, if you allow nipping and chewing to continue, just think about the damage that a mature Australian Kelpie can do with a full set of adult teeth.

Whenever your puppy nips your hand or fingers, cry out "Ouch!" in a loud voice, which should startle your puppy and stop him from nipping, even if only for a moment. Immediately distract him by offering a small treat or an appropriate toy for him to chew instead (which means having chew toys and puppy treats handy or in your pockets at all times). Praise him when he takes the toy and tell him what a good fellow he is. Praise is just as or even more important in puppy training as discipline and correction.

An important lesson for the Kelpie is to sink his teeth into his toys, not people's heels and ankles.

quite painful and a child's frightened reaction will only encourage a puppy to nip harder, which is a natural canine response. As with all other puppy situations, interaction between your Australian Kelpie puppy and children should be supervised.

Chewing on objects, not just family members' fingers and ankles, is also normal canine behavior that can be especially tedious (for the owner, not the pup) during the teething period when the puppy's adult teeth are coming in. At this stage, chewing just plain feels good. Furniture legs and cabinet corners are common puppy favorites. Shoes and other personal items also taste pretty good to a pup.

Puppies also tend to nip at children more often than adults, since they perceive little ones to be more vulnerable and more similar to their littermates. Teach your children appropriate responses to nipping behavior. If they are unable to handle it themselves, you may have to intervene. Puppy nips can be

The best solution is, once again, prevention. If you value something, keep it tucked away and out of reach. You can't hide

EASY, COWBOY!

Who's going to convince your dog that his rawhide toy isn't food? Dogs love rawhide and usually masticate the hide until it's soft enough to swallow. This can lead to choking or intestinal blockage, which is thankfully not terribly common. Another possible danger of rawhide results from the hides used in certain countries. Foreign hides can contain arsenic, lead, antibiotics or *Salmonella bacilli*. Even though imported chews are usually cheaper than American-made chews, this is one example in which buying American really counts.

Owners must carefully observe their dogs when they are chewing rawhide and remove any soft pieces that the dog pulls from the hide. Despite these drawbacks, rawhide chews do offer some benefits. Chewing rawhide can help keep the dog's teeth clean and distract your dog from chewing on your favorite leather loafers or sofa.

your dining-room table in a closet, but you can try to deflect the chewing by applying a bitter product made just to deter dogs from chewing. This spray-on substance is vile-tasting, although safe for dogs, and most puppies will avoid the forbidden object after one tiny taste. You also can apply the product to your leash if the puppy tries to chew on his lead during leash-training sessions.

Keep a ready supply of safe chews handy to offer your Australian Kelpie as a distraction when he starts to chew on something that's a "no-no." Remember, at this tender age, he does not yet know what is permitted or forbidden, so you have to be "on call" every minute he's awake and on the prowl.

You may lose a treasure or two during your puppy's growing-up period, and the furniture could sustain a nasty nick or two. These can be trying times, so be prepared for those

Sniffing and posturing are parts of the "get-to-know-you" ritual between dogs.

inevitable accidents and comfort yourself in knowing that this too shall pass.

JUMPING UP

All puppies jump up—on you, your guests, your counters and your furniture. Just another normal part of growing up, and one you need to meet head-on before it becomes an ingrained habit. The key to jump correction is consistency. You cannot correct your Australian Kelpie for jumping up on you today, then allow it to happen tomorrow by greeting him with hugs and kisses. As you have learned by now, consistency is critical to all puppy lessons.

For starters, try turning your back as soon as the puppy jumps. Jumping up is a means of gaining your attention and, if the pup can't see your face, he may get discouraged and learn that he loses eye contact with his beloved master when he jumps up.

Leash corrections also work, and most puppies respond well to a leash tug if they jump. Grasp the leash close to the puppy's collar and give a quick tug downward, using the command "Off." Do not use the word "Down," since "Down" is used to teach the puppy to lie down, which is a separate action that he will learn during his education in the basic

commands. As soon as the puppy has backed off, tell him to sit and immediately praise him for doing so. This will take many repetitions and won't be accomplished quickly, so don't get discouraged or give up; you must be even more persistent than your puppy.

A second method used for jump correction is the spritzer bottle. Fill a spray bottle with water mixed with a bit of lemon juice or vinegar. As soon as puppy jumps, command him "Off" and spritz him with the water mixture. Of course, that means having the spray bottle handy whenever or wherever jumping usually happens.

Yet a third method to discourage jumping is grasping the puppy's paws and holding them gently but firmly until he struggles to get away. Wait a brief moment or two, then release his paws and give him a command to sit. He should eventually learn that jumping gets him into an uncomfortable predicament.

Children are major victims of puppy jumping, since puppies view little people as ready targets for jumping up as well as nipping. If your children (or their friends) are unable to dispense jump corrections, you will have to intervene and handle it for them.

Important to prevention is

Make sure that all pets are secured *inside* your vehicle before hitting the open road.

FIRST CAR RIDE

The ride to your home from the breeder will likely be your puppy's first automobile experience, and you should make every effort to keep him comfortable and secure. Bring a large towel or small blanket for the puppy to lie on during the trip and an extra towel in case the pup gets carsick or has a potty accident. It's best to have another person with you to hold the puppy in his lap. Most puppies will fall fast asleep from the rolling motion of the car. If the ride is lengthy, you may have to stop so that the puppy can relieve himself, so be sure to bring a leash and collar for those stops. Avoid rest areas for potty trips, since those are frequented by many dogs, who may carry parasites or disease. It's better to stop at grassy areas near gas stations or shopping centers to prevent unhealthy exposure for your pup.

also knowing what you should not do. Never kick your Australian Kelpie (for any reason, not just for jumping) or knock him in the chest with your knee. That maneuver could actually harm your puppy. Vets can tell you stories about puppies who suffered broken bones after being banged about when they jumped up.

PUPPY WHINING

Puppies often cry and whine, just as infants and little children do. It's their way of telling us that they are lonely or in need of attention. Your puppy will miss his littermates and will feel insecure when he is left alone. You may be out of the house or just in another room, but he will still feel alone. During these times, the puppy's crate should be his personal comfort station, a place all his own where he can feel safe and secure. Once he learns that being alone is okay and not something to be feared, he will settle down without crying or objecting. You might want to leave a radio on while he is crated, as the sound of human voices can be soothing and will give the impression that people are around.

Give your puppy a favorite cuddly toy or chew toy to entertain him whenever he is crated. You will both be happier:

This multi-Kelpie family is happy with their own little herd of herders.

the puppy because he is safe in his den and you because he is quiet, safe and not getting into puppy escapades that can wreak havoc in your house or cause him danger.

To make sure that your puppy will always view his crate as a safe and cozy place, never, ever use the crate as punishment. That's the best way to turn the crate into a negative place that the pup will want to avoid. Sure, you can use the crate for your own peace of mind if your puppy is getting into trouble and needs some "time out." Just don't let him know that. Never scold the pup and immediately place him into the crate. Count to ten, give him a couple of hugs and maybe a treat, then scoot him into his crate.

It's also important not to make a big fuss when he is released from the crate. That will make getting out of the crate more appealing than being in the crate, which is just the opposite of what you are trying to achieve.

AUSTRALIAN KELPIE

FEEDING THE KELPIE

Before bringing your new puppy home with you, talk to the breeder about feeding. Most breeders provide new owners with diet sheets, detailing the kind of food the puppy has been eating, the number of feedings per day and the amount of food per meal. This regimen should be replicated as closely as possible. Feeding different brands of food or feeding too often or too much can cause an upset stomach and/or diarrhea. Likewise, the puppy's feeding schedule is a familiar routine to him, and sticking to it will help avoid stress and help the puppy make a smooth transition to your home.

Water should be available to your pup at all times during the day. At night, however, it's wise to restrict water consumption to a few sips after the last meal of the day. You won't want to get up too often for potty trips during the night because you allowed the puppy to drink too much water after dinner. For the adult dog, water should always be accessible. Your Kelpie will be active all day long and will need to replenish and rehydrate throughout the day as needed.

Feed the puppy from his own bowl and always in the same location, such as the corner of the kitchen, where you can watch him. Put his food bowl down, walk away and allow him 20 minutes to eat. At the end of that time, remove the bowl and don't offer food again until the next

Quality food, a basic grooming routine and plenty of activity are three important components of maintaining a happy and healthy Kelpie.

scheduled mealtime. Never feed him from your table!

Having a puppy that goes to his food bowl, nibbles a few pieces and walks away, only to return an hour later, means that you will be raising a dog that has no scheduled mealtime. If the dog gets sick, it may be some time before you realize that he's not feeling well because you don't realize that he's not eating properly. By putting his meal down and allowing him a few minutes to eat, you can tell immediately if he's feeling well or not. If he stays in place and finishes his meal without wandering around, you can be sure he's hungry and eager to eat. If he doesn't eat with enthusiasm, then you know that something's wrong. In that case, keep a sharp eye on him to see if he shows further signs of being unwell such as diarrhea, vomiting, listlessness and turning away from his next meal. Those are all signs that your vet should see him as soon as possible. Puppies are like little children when it comes to sickness—they can go downhill fast, but they also recuperate quickly. Dehydration is a major concern with puppies, so watch the puppy closely to be certain he's drinking water as he normally does.

For the first year of life, your puppy should be fed a quality puppy food. At around the age of one year, he should be switched to an active adult food. This is the food that he will continue to eat for most of his life. If the Kelpie is a working Kelpie, you should discuss with your breeder the amount and type of adult food that your dog will require to maintain energy and strength for long working hours. A good food

DIET DON'TS

- Got milk? Don't give it to your dog! Dogs cannot tolerate large quantities of cows' milk, as they do not have the enzymes to digest lactose.
- You may have heard of dog owners who add raw eggs to their dogs' food for a shiny coat or to make the food more palatable, but consumption of raw eggs too often can cause a deficiency of the vitamin biotin.
- Avoid feeding table scraps, as they will upset the balance of the dog's complete food. Additionally, fatty or highly seasoned foods can cause upset canine stomachs.
- Do not offer raw meat to your dog. Raw meat can contain parasites; it also is high in fat.
- Vitamin A toxicity in dogs can be caused by too much raw liver, especially if the dog already gets enough vitamin A in his balanced diet, which should be the case.
- Bones like chicken, pork chop and other soft bones are not suitable, as they easily splinter.

Feeding a hungry litter is no small task for this Kelpie mom.

food can be introduced to a dog at six or seven years of age, providing his activity level has with quality nutrition is important. Very active dogs like the Kelpie have different nutritional requirements than most dogs that get average amounts of exercise. Senior dog

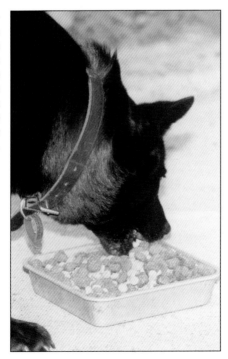

A quality adult-formula food with adequate nutrition for active dogs should maintain your Kelpie in good health. Ask your vet for advice about feeding your active Kelpie.

THE FIRST WEEKS

Puppies instinctively want to suck milk from their mother's teats; a normal puppy will exhibit this behavior just a few moments following birth. If puppies do not attempt to suckle within the first half-hour or so, they should be encouraged to do so by placing them on the nipples, having selected ones with plenty of milk. This early milk supply is important in providing the essential colostrum, which protects the puppies during the first eight to ten weeks of their lives. Although a mother's milk is much better than any commercially prepared milk formula, despite there being some excellent ones available, if the puppies do not feed, the breeder will have to feed them by hand. For those with less experience, advice from a vet is important so that not only the right quantity of milk is fed but also that of correct quality, fed at suitably frequent intervals, usually every two hours during the first few days of life.

Puppies should be allowed to nurse from their mothers for about the first six weeks, although, starting around the third or fourth week, the breeder will begin to introduce small portions of suitable solid food. Most breeders like to introduce alternate milk and meat meals initially, building up to weaning time.

slowed down. If, however, the dog is still working, he should be kept on an active adult formula until he retires.

When feeding a commercially prepared dog food, no growth supplements should be added to the Kelpie puppy's diet. All leading major-brand dog foods are highly fortified and contain all the nutrients that your dog needs. Exceeding the amount of nutrients already present can cause nutritional imbalances and both skeletal and joint deformities. The same is true for the adult and senior diet. Dog foods should contain complete and balanced nutrition so, except in certain circumstances as advised by the vet, no supplementation is necessary and can actually prove harmful.

Most commercial foods manufactured for dogs meet nutrition standards and list the ingredients contained in the food on every package and container. The ingredients are listed in descending order, with the main ingredient listed first. Refined sugars are not a part of a canine's natural food acquisition, and canine teeth are not genetically disposed to handling these sugars. Thus do not feed your Kelpie sugar products and avoid products that contain sugar in any high degree. Likewise, avoid the temptation to give your Kelpie treats of "people food." These can upset a dog's stomach and, some,

such as chocolate, onions, grapes, raisins, nuts and quantities of garlic, are actually toxic to dogs.

Fresh water (which is just as essential to his diet as good nutrition) and a properly prepared,

QUENCHING HIS THIRST

Is your dog drinking more than normal and trying to lap up everything in sight? Excessive thirst has many different causes. Obvious causes for a dog's being thirstier than usual are hot weather and vigorous exercise. However, if your dog is drinking more for no apparent reason, you could have cause for concern. Serious conditions like kidney or liver disease, diabetes and various types of hormonal problems can all be indicated by excessive drinking. If you notice your dog's being excessively thirsty, contact your vet at once. Hopefully there will be a simpler explanation, but the earlier a serious problem is detected, the sooner it can be treated, with a better rate of cure.

EXERCISE AND PLAY

Before you bring your new puppy home, make some plans about how you'll give him the proper kind and amount of exercise. Exercise is something that cannot be stressed too much with this breed. Remember, Kelpies are energetic dogs, filled with a drive to move and be active for hours and hours on end. Hanging around the house with no mental or

The breeder starts the pups on solid food as part of the weaning process.

balanced diet containing the essential nutrients in correct proportions are all a healthy Kelpie needs. Dog foods come in many different varieties and formulations. A visit to your local market or pet-supply store will reveal how vast an array is out there. It's best to follow the advice of your breeder and/or vet.

Bring a bowl and water for your Kelpie wherever you go so that he's always able to quench his thirst.

SWITCHING FOODS

There are certain times in a dog's life when it becomes necessary to switch his food; for example, from puppy to adult food and then from adult to senior-dog food. Additionally, you may decide to feed your pup a different type of food from what he received from the breeder, and there may be "emergency" situations in which you can't find your dog's normal brand and have to offer something else temporarily. Anytime a change is made, for whatever reason, the switch must be done gradually. You don't want to upset the dog's stomach or end up with a picky eater who refuses to eat something new. A tried-and-true approach is, over the course of about a week, to mix a little of the new food in with the old, increasing the proportion of new to old as the days progress. At the end of the week, you'll be feeding his regular portions of the new food, and he will barely notice the change.

physical stimulation is a recipe for trouble, as a bored Kelpie is a destructive Kelpie—that you can count on! Of course, work, work and more work is the most appropriate exercise for the Kelpie, but, if you have taken one on as a pet, you should be planning to spend much of your day, every day, exercising and doing things with your dog.

For the puppy, plan on providing a variety of activities that will keep him busy and help him become a physically fit adult. Although these dogs operate on full speed throughout their entire lives, young dogs go through a period from about 8 to 18 months old in which they don't even seem to sleep! This is a particularly difficult time period for pet owners; unfortunately, many Kelpies at this stage of life are given up by pet owners who are not prepared to cope with the breed's requirements.

Nonetheless, puppies still are puppies and exercise never should be forced. If he stops and refuses to continue with whatever you are doing, take him home for a rest. Young muscles and bones cannot tolerate high stress. Therefore, getting puppies involved in physical activities

A historical photo of a Kelpie at work in New South Wales, Australia, aptly illustrates the energy level and physical ability of the breed.

should be limited to what the puppy can comfortably do. You'll find that each week he can cover more distance and exercise for longer times than he did the week before. Forced exercise is harmful to the pup's growing frame, so let him set his own limits (although the Kelpie has few limits when it comes to activity!). Once your Kelpie reaches a year of age, he's ready to take on the world!

Taking walks and playing games with you are activities that help you and your puppy build a bond of loyalty to each other. Giving the Kelpie the exercise he needs helps him to build muscle and strengthen his heart and lungs in preparation for strenuous activities.

Taking the puppy to a variety of different environments also strengthens your bond, providing essential socialization while giving him the chance to stretch his legs. Taking him to places (on his lead, of course) like shopping centers, parks, beaches and

> **THE BOVINE CANINE**
> Does your dog's grazing in the back yard have you wondering whether he's actually a farm animal in disguise? Many owners have noticed their dogs' eating grass and wonder why. It is thought that dogs might eat grass to settle their stomachs or to relieve upset tummies. Even cats have been known to eat grass for the same reasons. Stomach upset can be caused by various things, including poor digestion and parasites.
>
> Unfortunately, while the grass may make the dog feel better very temporarily, often they vomit shortly after eating it, as grass can be irritating to a dog's stomach lining. Even worse, who knows what he is ingesting along with the grass? He could be swallowing insects, germs or parasites, thus perpetuating the problem. Grass-eating should be discouraged when you catch the dog in the act, and a trip to the vet to determine the underlying cause is in order.

Young Kelpies should never be forced to exercise. Puppies naturally get plenty of exercise doing things like playing and exploring.

wooded trails introduces your pup to different sights, sounds and smells that will help him develop self-confidence and trust in you. With Kelpies intended for work, ranchers will introduce their puppies to livestock.

One word of warning here: do not allow your puppy to jump until he's at least one year of age. Before that time, his bones are not

Taking a break for a belly rub! Plenty of activity and interaction with their owners make for content Kelpies.

fully developed and premature jumping could cause permanent damage to his bone growth.

Finally, encourage the puppy to play with all family members and friends. Exercising and playing with you and others helps to create a well-rounded individual with good physical and mental skills. It will also help him bond with each family member so that he will enjoy spending time with all of them. This helps the pet-owning family a great deal, as they can take turns with exercise each day—unless there is someone in the house that has six hours per day that he can devote to exercising the Kelpie!

When your Kelpie reaches adulthood, you can expand the types of exercise you do with him. Remember that this is a dog bred to work long hours (14-hour days!) over rough terrain, so he will be more than capable of outdistancing you on long walks, jogs and hikes. At the very least, a pet Kelpie will require three hours of exercise each day, preferably more. A few half-hour walks or Frisbee® sessions each day will not be enough, and you will be left with a hyperactive, frustrated, destructive dog. The pet owner can incorporate disc-catching and retrieving games as part of the dog's overall exercise program, but these things on their own are not sufficient.

Pet owners may want to try training for some type of canine sport. These dogs are not bred to be good obedience, agility or flyball dogs; they are bred for work, not competition. However, the bright and athletic Kelpie certainly has the potential to succeed in sports, so you may want to give one of these activities a try if your dog does not have the benefit of daily work. Be prepared, though—your Kelpie might not be as eager to partici-pate in competition as you are. Don't push it if your dog is disinterested.

GROOMING

All dogs need to be groomed; some more often than others. At the very least, every dog needs a clean coat, trimmed toenails, clean ears, healthy teeth and clear, bright eyes. The Kelpie's short coat is extremely easy to maintain. However, running through the brush and field can cause debris such as sticks, dead leaves, grass and other foreign matter to accumulate in the hair.

A soft bristle brush is the tool of choice to keep the Kelpie's coat free of foreign material. In addition, brushing the coat on a regular basis, once or twice a week, will keep the Kelpie's coat

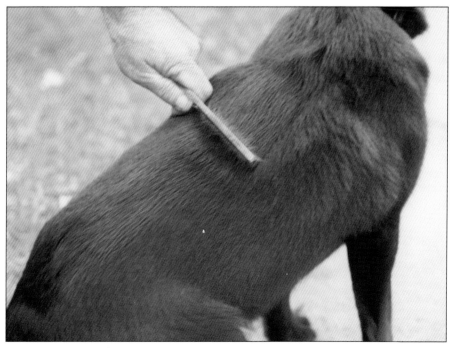

In addition to a soft bristle brush, a comb can be used to rid a Kelpie's coat of debris picked up outdoors.

SELECTING THE RIGHT BRUSHES AND COMBS

Will a rubber curry make my dog look slicker? Is a rake smaller than a pin brush? Do I choose nylon or natural bristles? Buying a dog brush can make the hairs on your head stand on end! Here's a quick once-over to educate you on the different types of brushes.

Slicker Brush: Fine metal prongs closely set on a curved base. Used to remove dead coat from the undercoat of medium- to long-coated breeds.

Pin Brush: Metal pins, often covered with rubber tips, set on an oval base. Used to remove shedding hair and is gentler than a slicker brush.

Metal Comb: Steel teeth attached to a steel handle; the closeness and size of the teeth vary greatly. A "flea comb" has tiny teeth set very closely together and is used to find fleas in a dog's coat. Combs with wider teeth are used for detangling longer coats.

Rake: Long-toothed comb with a short handle. Used to remove undercoat from heavily coated breeds with dense undercoats.

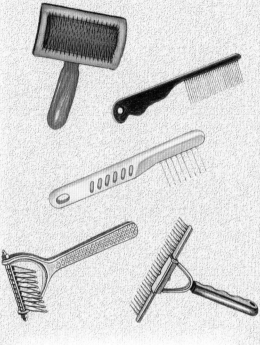

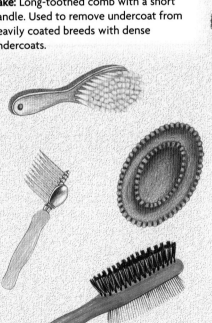

Soft-bristle Brush: Nylon or natural bristles set in a plastic or wood base. Used on short coats or long coats (without undercoats).

Rubber Curry: Rubber prongs, with or without a handle. Used for short-coated dogs. Good for use during shampooing.

Combination Brushes: Two-sided brush with a different type of bristle on each side; for example, pin brush on one side and slicker on the other, or bristle brush on one side and pin brush on the other. An economical choice if you need two kinds of brushes.

Grooming Glove: Sometimes called a hound glove; used to give sleek-coated dogs a once-over.

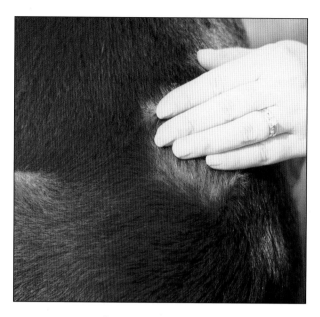

The Kelpie's coat is short, dense and flat, intended to protect the dog from the elements.

clinic. Another option is to take him to a groomer to have his nails trimmed. Whatever you decide, the puppy should learn early in life that nail trimming is a regular part of life that he must accept with tolerance.

If you decide to trim your Kelpie's nails yourself, here's an easy way to train your pup to enjoy his pedicures. Place the dog on a raised surface, such as a tabletop or on top of your washing machine, providing a rubber mat on which he can stand. The mat will provide traction for the dog so he won't slip and slide. Tell the puppy it's time to "Get pretty" and give him a small treat so he associates something pleasant with your "Get pretty" command.

Now take one front paw in your hand and clip one nail as your vet instructed. Immediately, put the clipper down and give the puppy a small treat while you tell him what a good boy he is. When he's finished eating the treat, clip one more nail and repeat the reward process, each time letting him know how special and wonderful he is as he shows you his paw. Use small treats or pieces of treats so that you're not overdoing it.

When you begin this training, clip only one foot at a time. Do the second foot the following day and the two back feet on the third and fourth days. That way, he won't lose patience with the

shiny and healthy. Every time you brush the dog, check his ears to be sure that they're clean and free of unwanted wax and foreign matter, and check his teeth and mouth. You can learn to brush your dog's teeth by asking the vet to show you how during one of your pup's early veterinary visits. The vet will either give you or recommend a toothbrush made for dogs (there are several types from which to choose) and a special toothpaste formulated for canines. Never use human toothpaste with your dog.

Trimming toenails is something else that you and your vet should discuss. Either you can ask the vet to teach you how to do it or you can have the vet trim your dog's nails there in the

THE MONTHLY GRIND

If your dog doesn't like the feeling of nail clippers or if you're not comfortable using them, you may wish to try an electric nail grinder. This tool has a small sandpaper disc on the end that rotates to grind the nails down. Some feel that using a grinder reduces the risk of cutting into the quick; this can be true if the tool is used properly. Usually you will be able to tell where the quick is before you get to it. A benefit of the grinder is that it creates a smooth finish on the nails so that there are no ragged edges.

Because the tool makes noise, your dog should be introduced to it before the actual grinding takes place. Turn it on and let your dog hear the noise; turn it off and let him inspect it with you holding it. Use the grinder gently, holding it firmly and progressing a little at a time until you reach the proper length. Look at the nail as you grind so that you do not go too short. Stop at any indication that you are nearing the quick. It will take a few sessions for both you and the puppy to get used to the grinder.

out the clippers and the biscuits, he'll run to the usual area in anticipation of his "Get pretty" time and the resulting treats and praise. Soon you'll be able to clip the nails on all four feet at one time without the pup giving it a second thought. At that point, you can reduce the frequency of the food treats and just reward him with one treat at the end of his pedicure.

Keeping the Kelpie's ears clean is easy. Use a cotton ball or soft tissue soaked in an ear-cleaning solution, available from your vet or a pet-supply store. Wipe only the surface you can reach with your finger and never probe down into the ear with your finger or anything else. If a bug or other matter gets down into the

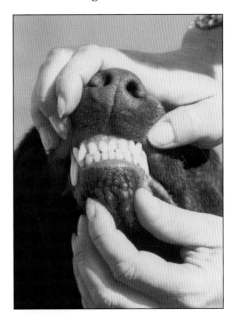

Clean, healthy teeth and gums are important to a dog's overall good condition.

process. The frequent rewards will keep him interested in the treats and not in the fact that you're holding his foot and clipping his nails.

You are teaching your puppy to look forward to nail-trimming time. Whenever he sees you get

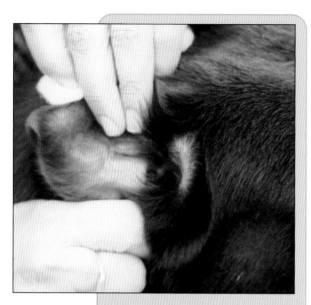

THE EARS KNOW

Examining your puppy's ears helps ensure good internal health. The ears are the eyes to the dog's innards! Begin handling your puppy's ears when he's still young so that he doesn't protest every time you lift a flap or touch his ears. Yeast and bacteria are two of the culprits that you can detect by examining the ear. You will notice a strong, often foul, odor, debris, redness or some kind of discharge. All of these point to health problems that can worsen over time. Additionally, you are on the lookout for wax accumulation, ear mites and other tiny bothersome parasites and their even tinier droppings. You may have to pluck hair with tweezers in order to have a better view into the dog's ears, but this is painless if done carefully.

ear canal, do not try to dig it out. Take your dog to the vet as soon as possible so it can be removed safely without damaging the canal or eardrum. Also be on the lookout for dark-brown droppings or unusual odor, which indicate ear-mite infestation or other types of infection.

Occasionally foreign matter will collect in the corners of your dog's eyes. You can remove it by wiping the corners with a soft cloth or tissue moistened with pure water. If you see a yellowish substance coming from the eye or if you see the dog rubbing his eye on soft surfaces such as a carpet, have your veterinarian examine the eye for foreign matter and/or infection.

Kelpies do not need to be bathed very often. Occasionally your Kelpie will get into something that needs to be washed out, or sometimes his coat just needs refreshing after a particularly heavy period of shedding. When it's time for a bath, there are several simple steps to a quick and easy bath experience.

First of all, as with most grooming activities, make bathing fun for your Kelpie. A happy tone of voice when you begin, praising the dog for being so good while you're bathing him and rewarding him with a biscuit when you're done will soon have the dog coming freely to you

shiny, clean coat. Brisk towel-drying is all that will be necessary. Use as many dry towels as necessary to get the coat as close to dry as possible. Blow-drying the coat with a hair dryer isn't needed for short-coated breeds as long as they're thoroughly towel-dried. Just make sure that the dog stays out of drafts and away from cold air until he's completely dry.

If your Kelpie gets paint or tar-type substances on his coat, apply a liberal amount of mineral oil to the area. Let the oil soak in for

The Kelpie's short coat is easy to maintain, but don't forget other important aspects of the total grooming routine, including toothbrushing, nail clipping and care of the eyes and ears.

when you tell him, "It's bath time!"

Use a regular dog shampoo (never one made for human hair) and warm water. Wet the dog down, apply the shampoo and rub it into a lather in the same way that you shampoo your own hair. Make sure you get the shampoo all the way down to his skin, not just on the surface of the coat.

Rinse thoroughly with clear water. Be sure to rinse well, as leaving a residue of shampoo on his skin can cause painful irritation and burning. A few extra minutes of rinsing will keep the dog comfortable and produce a

WATER SHORTAGE

No matter how well behaved your dog is, bathing is always a project! Nothing can substitute for a good warm bath, but owners do have the option of giving their dogs "dry" baths. Pet shops sell excellent products, in both powder and spray forms, designed for spot-cleaning your dog. These dry shampoos are convenient for touch-up jobs when you don't have the time to bathe your dog in the traditional way.

Muddy feet, messy behinds and smelly coats can be spot-cleaned and deodorized with a "wet-nap"-style cleaner. On those days when your dog insists on rolling in fresh goose droppings and there's no time for a bath, a spot bath can save the day. These pre-moistened wipes are also handy for other grooming needs like wiping faces, ears and eyes and freshening tails and behinds.

SCOOTING HIS BOTTOM

Here's a doggy problem that many owners tend to neglect. If your dog is scooting his rear end around the carpet, he probably is experiencing anal-sac impaction or blockage. The anal sacs are the two grape-sized glands on either side of the dog's vent. The dog cannot empty these glands, which become filled with a foul-smelling material. The dog may attempt to lick the area to relieve the pressure. He may also rub his anus on your walls, furniture or floors.

Don't neglect your dog's rear end during grooming sessions. By squeezing both sides of the anus with a soft cloth, you can express some of the material in the sacs. If the material is pasty and thick, you likely will need the assistance of a veterinarian. Vets know how to express the glands and can show you how to do it correctly without hurting the dog or spraying yourself with the unpleasant liquid.

about ten minutes and then rub briskly with an absorbent cloth. Follow with a good bath. Never use strong chemicals on your dog, as irritations to the skin will cause the dog to suffer and will require veterinary attention.

IDENTIFICATION AND TRAVEL

ID FOR YOUR DOG

You love your Australian Kelpie and want to keep him safe. Of course you take every precaution to prevent his escaping from the yard or becoming lost or stolen. You have a sturdy high fence and you always keep your dog on lead when out and about in public places. If your dog is not properly identified, however, you are overlooking a major aspect of his safety. We hope to never be in a situation where our dog is missing, but we should practice prevention in the unfortunate case that this happens; identification greatly increases the chances of your dog's being returned to you.

There are several ways to identify your dog. First, the traditional dog tag should be a staple in your dog's wardrobe, attached to his everyday collar. Tags can be made of sturdy plastic and various metals and should include your contact information so that a person who finds the dog can get in touch with you right away to arrange his return. Many people today enjoy the wide range of decorative tags available, so have fun and create a tag to match your dog's personality. Of course, it is important that the tag stays on the collar, so have a secure "O" ring attachment; you also can explore the type of tag that slides right onto the collar.

In addition to the ID tag, which every dog should wear even if identified by another method, two other forms of identi-fication have become popular:

a company with a universal microchip that can be read by scanners made by other companies as well. It won't do any good to have the dog chipped if the information cannot be retrieved. Also, not every humane society, shelter and clinic is equipped with a scanner, although more and more facilities are equipping themselves. In fact, many shelters microchip dogs that they adopt out to new homes.

Because the microchip is not visible to the eye, the dog must wear a tag that states that he is microchipped so that whoever picks him up will know to have him scanned. The microchip tag usually also includes the dog's microchip ID number and the registry's phone number. He of course also should have a tag with your contact information in case

Your dog's ID tags should contain your contact information and should be securely fastened to his everyday collar.

microchipping and tattooing. In microchipping, a tiny scannable chip is painlessly inserted under the dog's skin. The number is registered to you so that, if your lost dog turns up at a clinic or shelter, the chip can be scanned to retrieve your contact information.

The advantage of the microchip is that it is a permanent form of ID, but there are some factors to consider. Several different companies make microchips, and not all are compatible with the others' scanning devices. It's best to find

PET OR STRAY?

Besides the obvious benefit of providing your contact information to whoever finds your lost dog, an ID tag makes your dog more approachable and more likely to be recovered. A strange dog wandering the neighborhood without a collar and tags will look like a stray, while the collar and tags indicate that the dog is someone's pet. Even if the ID tags become detached from the collar, the collar alone will make a person more likely to pick up the dog.

his chip information cannot be retrieved. Humane societies and veterinary clinics offer this service, which is usually very affordable.

Though less popular than microchipping, tattooing is another permanent method of ID for dogs. Most vets perform this service, and there are also clinics that perform dog tattooing. This is also an affordable procedure and one that will not cause much discomfort for the dog. It is best to put the tattoo in a visible area, such as the ear, to deter theft. It is sad to say that there are cases of dogs' being stolen and sold to research laboratories, but such laboratories will not accept tattooed dogs.

To ensure that the tattoo is effective in aiding your dog's return to you, the tattoo number must be registered with a national organization. That way, when someone finds a tattooed dog, a phone call to the registry will quickly match the dog with his owner.

HIT THE ROAD

Car travel with your Australian Kelpie may be limited to necessity only, such as trips to the vet, or you may bring your dog along almost everywhere you go. This will depend much on your individual dog and how he reacts to rides in the car. You can begin desensitizing your dog to car travel as a pup so that it's something that he's used to. Still, some dogs suffer from motion sickness. Your vet may prescribe a medication for this if trips in the car pose a problem for your dog. At the very least, you will need to get him to the vet, so he will need to tolerate these trips with the least amount of hassle possible.

Start taking your pup on short trips, maybe just around the block to start. If he is fine with short trips, lengthen your rides a little at a time. Start to take him on your errands or just for drives around town. By this time it will be easy to tell whether your dog is a born traveler or would prefer staying at home when you are on the road.

Of course, safety is a concern for dogs in the car. First, he must travel securely, not left loose to roam about the car where he could be injured or distract the driver. A young pup can be held by a passenger initially but should soon graduate to a travel crate, which can be the same crate he uses in the home. Other options include a car harness (like a seat belt for dogs) and partitioning the back of the car with a gate made for this purpose.

Bring along what you will need for the dog. He should wear his collar and ID tags, of course, and you should bring his leash, water (and food if a long trip) and clean-up materials for potty breaks and in case of motion sickness.

Always keep your dog on his leash when you make stops, and never leave him alone in the car. Many a dog has died from the heat inside a closed car; this does not take much time at all. A dog left alone inside a car can also be a target for thieves.

Research boarding facilities in your area well in advance of needing to board your dog. You want to be confident about the care that your Kelpie will receive while you are away.

BOARDING

Today there are many options for dog owners who need someone to care for their dogs in certain circumstances. While many think of boarding their dogs as something to do when away on vacation, many others use the services of doggie "daycare" facilities, dropping their dogs off to spend the day while they are at work. Many of these facilities offer both long-term and daily care. Many go beyond just boarding and cater to all sorts of needs, with on-site grooming, veterinary care, training classes and even "web-cams" where owners can log onto the Internet and check out what their dogs are up to. Most dogs enjoy the activity and time spent with other dogs.

Before you need to use such a service, check out the ones in your area. Make visits to see the facilities, meet the staff, discuss fees and available services and see whether this is a place where you think your dog will be happy. It is best to do your research in advance so that you're not stuck at the last minute, forced into making a rushed decision without knowing whether the kennel that you've chosen meets your standards. You also can check with your vet's office to see whether they offer boarding for their clients or can recommend a good kennel in the area.

The kennel will need to see proof of your dog's health records and vaccinations so as not to spread illness from dog to dog. Your dog also will need proper identification. Owners usually experience some separation anxiety the first time they have to leave their dog in someone else's care, so it's reassuring to know that the kennel you choose is run by experienced, caring, true dog people.

AUSTRALIAN KELPIE

This chapter will discuss two vital topics related to your Australian Kelpie's education: house-training and obedience training. Following these discussions are some training tips and activities to keep your Kelpie active and happy. Kelpies are bright, intuitive dogs

"What does a puppy have to do to get some privacy around here?"

THE RIGHT START

The best advice for a potential dog owner is to start with the very best puppy that money can buy. Don't shop around for a bargain in the newspaper. You're buying a companion, not a used car or a second-hand appliance. The purchase price of the dog represents a very significant part of the investment, but this is indeed a very small sum compared to the expenses of maintaining the dog in good health. If you purchase a well-bred healthy and sound puppy, you will be starting right. An unhealthy puppy can cost you thousands of dollars in unnecessary veterinary expenses and, possibly, a fortune in heartbreak as well.

and can be compared to the famous canine Rhodes Scholar, the Border Collie, arguably the brightest of the bright. Unlike Border Collies, however, Kelpies don't thrive on obedience training and like to know why they are being asked to jump through the hoop. Kelpies like to think for themselves, often taking their own initiatives, and despise endless

Is there any doubt, looking at this Kelpie's face, that this is a bright and alert breed?

All members of the family (young and old) should participate in training your Kelpie.

effortlessly, may make a new owner believe that training the Kelpie is an easy task. The author assures you, it absolutely is not. Training a Kelpie requires 100% commitment on the part of the trainer, which is a reasonable contribution since the Kelpie is willing to give 200%—8 to 10 hours a day! A trainer must be patient, dog-smart and consistent if he expects to properly educate his Kelpie. Whether for stockdog work, basic obedience lessons or something as elementary as house-training, you need to be on your toes and ready for work. Much of your dog's obedience training is done by you, his owner, practicing lessons every day.

Even for Kelpie owners who enroll their dogs in obedience classes, practice at home is vital to success in training. The instructor of an obedience class and the presence of other owners and their dogs will add to your dog's socialization experiences while teaching him basic behaviors. The class is helpful for you, too. You will be able to teach your dog good manners as you learn how and why he behaves the way he does. You will find out how to communicate with your dog and how to recognize and understand his communications with you.

Those involved with teaching dog obedience and counseling owners about their dogs' behavior have discovered some interesting facts about dog ownership. For

repetition of commands. They are practical dogs: "I just sat for you. Why should I do it again and again? Make up your mind."

Kelpie owners must be very firm with their dogs and always fair. You must earn your Kelpie's respect; once it's gained, he will regard you as the top dog, the almighty "alpha" canine of the house. If he sees you falter (by repeating boring commands or giving unclear directions), he may attempt to assume the role of top dog himself (since you apparently don't deserve the designation, in his eyes).

Watching a working Kelpie performing the role of stockdog on a herd of sheep, flawlessly and

SHOULD WE ENROLL?

If you have the means and the time, you should definitely take your dog to obedience classes. Begin with puppy kindergarten classes in which puppies of all sizes learn basic lessons while getting the opportunity to meet and greet each other; it's as much about socialization as it is about good manners. What you learn in class you can practice at home. And if you goof up in practice, you'll get help in the next session.

example, training dogs when they are puppies results in the highest rate of success in developing well-mannered and well-adjusted adult dogs. Training an older dog, from six months to six years of age, can produce almost equal results, providing that the owner accepts the dog's slower rate of learning capability and is willing to work patiently to help the dog succeed at developing to his fullest potential. Unfortunately, many owners of untrained adult dogs lack the patience factor, so they do not persist until their dogs are successful at learning particular behaviors.

The best way is to begin training right away, before your Kelpie develops his own bad habits. Once a Kelpie develops these bad habits, and his own way of thinking, it will be immeasurably difficult to break him. Kelpies

can be a bit "cow-headed." This is especially true of young dogs that are introduced to stock. Some trainers simply throw the dog into the yard and expect him to "work." While instinct plays a significant part in the work of a stockdog, there's a lot of craft and technique that require training. If the young dog starts biting or rushing the animals, it may be all but impossible to correct these kind of bad habits.

Training a puppy aged 10 to 16 weeks (20 weeks at the most) is like working with a dry sponge in a pool of water. The pup soaks up whatever you show him and constantly looks for more things to do and learn. At this early age, his

Training your Kelpie goes beyond commands and tasks to teaching him good manners, such as how to behave (and how *not* to behave) at mealtimes.

body is not yet producing hormones, and therein lies the reason for such a high rate of success. Without hormones, he is focused on his owner and not particularly interested in investigating other places, dogs, people, etc. You are the alpha leader: his provider of food, water, shelter and security. He latches onto you and wants to stay close. He will usually follow you from room to room, will not let you out of his sight when you are outdoors with him and will respond in like manner to the people and animals you encounter. If you greet a friend warmly, he will be happy to greet the person as well. If, however, you are hesitant or anxious about the approach of a stranger, he will likely respond accordingly.

Once the puppy begins to produce hormones, his natural curiosity emerges and he begins to investigate the world around him. It is at this time when you may notice that the untrained dog begins to wander away from you and even ignore your commands to stay close. When this behavior becomes a problem, you have two choices: get rid of the dog or train him. It is strongly urged that you choose the latter option.

Most likely you will be able to find reasonably priced obedience classes in your area. At home, too, you will want to reinforce your Kelpie's ever-growing education with some

A Kelpie can learn quickly how to fetch a ball and will enjoy such interactive games with you.

"homework." Every instructor teaches the basic commands somewhat differently, but all approaches generally revolve around the simple principles of positive reinforcement. Kelpies respond best to inducive training and lots of "Good dog" praise. Now let us get started with some basic training for the home.

HOUSE-TRAINING YOUR KELPIE

House-training is an important issue with all dogs, especially puppies. You can train a puppy to relieve himself wherever you choose, but this must be somewhere suitable. You should bear in mind from the outset that

OUR CANINE KIDS

"Everything I learned about parenting, I learned from my dog." How often adults recognize that their parenting skills are mere extensions of the education they acquired while caring for their dogs. Many owners refer to their dogs as their "kids" and treat their canine companions like real members of the family. Surveys indicate that a majority of dog owners talk to their dogs regularly, celebrate their dogs' birthdays and purchase Christmas gifts for their dogs. Another survey shows that dog owners take their dogs to the veterinarian more frequently than they visit their own physicians.

when your puppy is old enough to go out in public places, any canine deposits must be picked up at once. You will always have to carry with you a small plastic bag or "pooper-scooper."

Outdoor training includes such surfaces as grass, soil and cement. Indoor training, which is not an option for a dog the size of the Kelpie, usually means training your dog to newspaper. When deciding on the surface and location that you will want your Kelpie to use, be sure it is going to be permanent. Training your dog to grass and then changing your mind a few months later is extremely difficult for both dog and owner.

Kelpies are not typically dog-aggressive and they enjoy meeting new people, so socialization should be fun for both of you.

SOMEBODY TO BLAME

House-training a puppy can be frustrating for the puppy and the owner alike. The puppy does not instinctively understand the difference between defecating on the pavement outside and on the ceramic tile in the kitchen. He is confused and frightened by his human's exuberant reactions to his natural urges. The owner, arguably the more intelligent of the duo, is also frustrated that he cannot convince his puppy to obey his commands and instructions.

In frustration, the owner may struggle with the temptation to discipline the puppy, scold him or even strike him on the rear end. Harsh corrections are unnecessary and inappropriate, serving to defeat your purpose in gaining your puppy's trust and respect. Don't blame your nine-week-old puppy. Blame yourself for not being 100% consistent in the puppy's lessons and routine. The lesson here is simple: try harder and your puppy will succeed.

Next, choose the command you will use each and every time you want your puppy to void. "Hurry up" and "Let's go" are examples of commands commonly used by dog owners. Get in the habit of giving the puppy your chosen relief command before you take him out. That way, when he becomes an adult, you will be able to determine if he wants to go out when you ask him. A confirmation will be signs of interest, such as wagging his tail, watching you intently, going to the door, etc.

Puppy's Needs

Your puppy needs to relieve himself after play periods, after each meal, after he has been sleeping and at any time he indicates that he is looking for a place to urinate or defecate. The urinary and intestinal tract muscles of very young puppies are not fully developed. Therefore, like human babies, puppies need to relieve themselves frequently.

Take your puppy out often—every hour for an eight-week-old, for example—and always immediately after sleeping and eating. The older the puppy, the less often he will need to relieve himself. Finally, as a mature healthy adult, he will require only three to five relief trips per day.

The Crate

When you bring your new little mate home, you should have a crate ready. Contrary to those who believe that crate training is cruel and dogs should be given the run of the house, crate training your puppy is an extremely positive way of controlling your dog, housebreaking the puppy, protecting your home and possessions and keeping the puppy safe from serious (even fatal!) accidents.

Imagine, if you will, that you find yourself at dusk in an empty football stadium. Someone tells you to spend the night there alone and they'll come back for you at dawn. The very thought of staying in such a vast, open area alone would be enough to put you in a panic. The fact that you're all alone in a huge, open place would be traumatic. That's exactly how your puppy will feel if you allow him the run of the whole house or even a large room. He would be traumatized by the immensity of the place and the fact that there's no place for him to lie down and rest securely.

Like the dog in the wild, your puppy needs a private, secure, small area where he can rest in safety. Giving the puppy his own crate provides him with a warm,

The crate should provide your Kelpie with a place of comfort and retreat. He should always associate the crate with positive experiences.

comfortable place of security in which he can sleep without being disturbed by elements in his environment such as children, other pets, people moving around, etc. In the wild, for example, dogs and other creatures find tiny spaces hidden from view in which to rest securely away from outside threats to their safety. A wild dog will choose a space that is just big enough for him to curl up and lie down. The space will enclose the dog from the sides and above, leaving just enough open space for him to use as an entrance and exit.

A crate, therefore, should be similar to the "cubbyhole" space chosen by the wild dog. It should be big enough for the puppy to lie down, stretch out and turn around yet small enough so he will not want to urinate or defecate in it,

BASIC PRINCIPLES OF DOG TRAINING

1. Start training early. A young puppy is ready, willing and able.
2. Timing is your all-important tool. Praise at the exact time that the dog responds correctly. Pay close attention.
3. Patience is almost as important as timing!
4. Repeat! The same word has to mean the same thing every time.
5. In the beginning, praise all correct behavior verbally, along with treats and petting.

because dogs do not like to soil their sleeping areas. It should also be tall enough that he can stand without rubbing his head on the top. It's better to purchase a crate that will accommodate the full-size adult Kelpie than to invest in two crates, one for the puppy and one for the adult. You can use a partition in the adult-sized crate so that the puppy does not have access to the whole crate. You are trying to make him comfortable while avoiding his sleeping in one corner and eliminating in the other. As the puppy grows, you can remove the partition.

The dog's crate should contain clean bedding and a sturdy toy. Avoid putting food or water in the dog's crate before he is fully house-trained, as eating and drinking will activate his digestive processes and ultimately defeat your purpose, not to mention make the puppy very uncomfort-

able if he always has "to go." Once house-training has been achieved reliably, water must be made available in his area, in a non-spill container.

CONTROL
By control, we mean helping the puppy to create a lifestyle pattern that will be compatible to that of his human pack (you!). Just as we guide little children to learn our way of life, we must show the puppy when it is time to play, eat, sleep, exercise and even entertain himself. Your puppy should always sleep in his crate. He should also learn that, during times of household confusion and excessive human activity, such as at breakfast when family members are preparing for the day, he can play by himself in relative safety and comfort in his designated area. Each time you leave the puppy alone, he should understand exactly where he is to stay.

Likewise, accustoming the pup to his crate not only keeps him safe but also avoids his engaging in destructive behaviors when you are not around. Let's face it, all puppies are chewers and they cannot tell the difference between a safe chew toy, your leather shoes and a dangerous electrical wire. Chewing into a live wire, for example, can be fatal to the puppy, while a shorted wire can start a fire in the house.

CANINE DEVELOPMENT SCHEDULE

It is important to understand how and at what age a puppy develops into adulthood. If you are a puppy owner, consult this Canine Development Schedule to determine the stage of development your puppy is currently experiencing. This knowledge will help you as you work with the puppy in the weeks and months ahead.

PERIOD	AGE	CHARACTERISTICS
FIRST TO THIRD	BIRTH TO SEVEN WEEKS	Puppy needs food, sleep and warmth and responds to simple and gentle touching. Needs mother for security and disciplining. Needs littermates for learning and interacting with other dogs. Pup learns to function within a pack and learns pack order of dominance. Begin socializing pup with adults and children for short periods. Pup begins to become aware of his environment.
FOURTH	EIGHT TO TWELVE WEEKS	Brain is fully developed. Pup needs socializing with outside world. Remove from mother and littermates. Needs to change from canine pack to human pack. Human dominance necessary. Fear period occurs between 8 and 12 weeks. Avoid fright and pain.
FIFTH	THIRTEEN TO SIXTEEN WEEKS	Training and formal obedience should begin. Less association with other dogs, more with people, places, situations. Period will pass easily if you remember this is pup's change-to-adolescence time. Be firm and fair. Flight instinct prominent. Permissiveness and over-disciplining can do permanent damage. Praise for good behavior.
JUVENILE	FOUR TO EIGHT MONTHS	Another fear period about seven to eight months of age. It passes quickly, but be cautious of fright and pain. Sexual maturity reached. Dominant traits established. Dog should understand sit, down, come and stay by now.

NOTE: THESE ARE APPROXIMATE TIME FRAMES. ALLOW FOR INDIVIDUAL DIFFERENCES IN PUPPIES.

If the puppy chews up your favorite shoes (which you should not be leaving around, anyway!), you would probably discipline him angrily when you returned home. Thus he makes the association that your coming home means he is going to be punished. (He will not remember eating your shoes and is incapable of making the association of the discipline with his naughty deed.) Thus the crate is helpful for keeping the puppy both safe and out of trouble.

The crate is also useful for keeping the puppy from underfoot when things are getting too busy for the pup. Times of excitement, such as special occasions, family parties, etc., can still be fun for the puppy, providing that he can view the activities from the security of his designated area. He

DAILY SCHEDULE
How many relief trips does your puppy need per day? A puppy up to the age of 14 weeks will need to go outside about 8 to 12 times per day! You will have to take the pup out any time he starts sniffing around the floor or turning in small circles, as well as after naps, meals, games and lessons or whenever he's released from his crate. Once the puppy is 14 to 22 weeks of age, he will require only 6 to 8 relief trips. At the ages of 22 to 32 weeks, the puppy will require about 5 to 7 trips. Adult dogs typically require 4 relief trips per day, in the morning, afternoon, evening and late at night.

is not underfoot and he is not being fed all sorts of tidbits that will probably cause him stomach distress, yet he still feels a part of the fun.

ESTABLISHING A SCHEDULE
A puppy should be taken to his relief area each time he is released from his crate, after meals, after a play session and when he first awakens in the morning (at age eight weeks, this can mean 5 A.M.!). The puppy will indicate that he's ready "to go" by circling or sniffing busily—do not misinterpret these signs. For a puppy less than eight or nine weeks of age, a routine of taking him out every hour is

The crate is a useful safety tool, as your Kelpie can be securely confined wherever you go if the need arises.

necessary. As the puppy grows, he will be able to wait for longer periods of time.

Keep trips to his relief area short. Stay no more than five or six minutes and then return to the house. If he goes during that time, praise him lavishly and take him indoors immediately. If he does not, but he has an accident when you go back indoors, pick him up immediately, say "No! No!" and return to his relief area. Wait a few minutes, then return to the house again. Never hit a puppy or rub his face in urine or excrement

THE SUCCESS METHOD

Success that comes by luck is usually short-lived. Success that comes by well-thought-out proven methods is often more easily achieved and permanent. This is the Success Method. It is designed to give you, the puppy owner, a simple yet proven way to help your puppy develop clean living habits and a feeling of security in his new environment.

6 STEPS TO SUCCESSFUL CRATE TRAINING

1 Tell the puppy "Crate time!" and place him into the crate with a small treat (a piece of cheese or half of a biscuit). Let him stay in the crate for five minutes while you are in the same room. Then release him and praise lavishly. Never release him when he is fussing. Wait until he is quiet before you let him out.

2 Repeat Step 1 several times a day.

3 The next day, place the puppy into the crate as before. Let him stay there for ten minutes. Do this several times.

4 Continue building time in five-minute increments until the puppy stays in his crate for 30 minutes with you in the room. Always take him to his relief area after prolonged periods in his crate.

5 Now go back to Step 1 and let the puppy stay in his crate for five minutes, this time while you are out of the room.

6 Once again, build crate time in five-minute increments with you out of the room. When the puppy will stay willingly in his crate (he may even fall asleep!) for 30 minutes with you out of the room, he will be ready to stay in it for several hours at a time.

when he has had an accident.

Once indoors, put the puppy in his crate until you have had time to clean up his accident. Then, release him to the family area and watch him more closely. Chances are his accident was a result of your not picking up his signal or waiting too long before offering him the opportunity to relieve himself. Never hold a grudge against the puppy for accidents.

Let the puppy learn that going outdoors means it is time to relieve himself, not to play. Once trained, he will be able to play indoors and out and still differentiate between the times for play versus the times for relief. Help him develop regular hours for

TIDY BOY

Clean by nature, dogs do not like to soil their dens, which in effect are their crates or sleeping quarters. Unless not feeling well, dogs will not defecate or urinate in their crates. Crate training capitalizes on the dog's natural desire to keep his den clean. Be conscientious about giving the puppy as many opportunities to relieve himself outdoors as possible. Reward the puppy for correct behavior. Praise him and pat him whenever he "goes" in the correct location. Even the tidiest of puppies can have potty accidents, so be patient and dedicate more energy to helping your puppy achieve a clean lifestyle.

This Kelpie has the routine down. He knows how to ask when its time to go out *and* come back in.

naps, being alone, playing by himself and just resting, all in his crate. Encourage him to entertain himself while you are busy with your activities. Let him learn that having you near is comforting, but it is not your main purpose in life to provide him with undivided attention. Each time you put your puppy in his own area, use the same command, whatever suits best. Soon he will run to his crate or special area when he hears you say those words.

Crate training provides safety for you, the puppy and the home. It also provides the puppy with a feeling of security, and that helps the puppy achieve self-confidence and clean habits. Remember that one of the primary ingredients in house-training your puppy is control. Regardless of your

lifestyle, there will always be occasions when you will need to have a place where your dog can stay and be happy and safe. Crate training is the answer for now and in the future.

In conclusion, a few key elements are really all you need for a successful house-training method—consistency, frequency, praise, control and supervision. By following these procedures with a normal, healthy puppy, you and the puppy will soon be past the stage of "accidents" and ready to move on to a clean and rewarding life together.

ROLES OF DISCIPLINE, REWARD AND PUNISHMENT

Discipline, training one to act in accordance with rules, brings order to life. It is as simple as that. Without discipline, particularly in a group society, chaos will reign supreme and the group will eventually perish. Humans and canines are social animals and need some form of discipline in order to function effectively. They must procure food, reproduce to keep their species going and protect their home base and their young. If there were no discipline in the lives of social animals, they would eventually die from starvation and/or predation by other stronger animals. In the case of domestic canines, discipline in their lives is needed in order for them to understand how their pack

CREATURES OF HABIT

Canine behaviorists and trainers aptly describe dogs as "creatures of habit," meaning that dogs respond to structure in their daily lives and welcome a routine. Do not interpret this to mean that dogs enjoy endless repetition in their training sessions. Dogs get bored just as humans do. Keep training sessions interesting and exciting. Vary the commands and the locations in which you practice. Give short breaks for play in between lessons. A bored student will never be the best performer in the class.

(you and other family members) functions and how they must act in order to survive.

Dr. Edward Thorndike, a world-famous animal psychologist, established *Thorndike's Theory of Learning*, which states that a behavior that results in a pleasant event tends to be repeated. Furthermore, it concludes that a behavior that results in an unpleasant event tends not to be repeated. It is this theory upon which training methods are based today. For example, if you manipulate a dog to perform a specific behavior and reward him for doing it, he is likely to do it again

WHO'S TRAINING WHOM?
Dog training is a black-and-white exercise. The correct response to a command must be absolute, and the trainer must insist on completely accurate responses from the dog. A trainer cannot command his dog to sit and then settle for the dog's melting into the down position. Often owners are so pleased that their dogs "did something" in response to a command that they just shrug and say, "OK, Down" even though they wanted the dog to sit. You want your dog to respond to the command without hesitation: he must respond at that moment and correctly every time.

Treats are used as rewards for a job well done. This Kelpie learns the sit command by being rewarded when he assumes the sit position.

because he enjoyed the end result.

Occasionally, punishment, a penalty inflicted for an offense, is necessary. The best type of punishment often comes from an outside source. For example, a child is told not to touch the oven because he may get burned. He disobeys and touches the oven. In doing so, he receives a burn. From that time on, he respects the heat of the oven and avoids contact with it. Therefore, a behavior that results in an unpleasant event tends not to be repeated.

A good example of a dog's learning the hard way is the dog who chases the house cat. He is told many times to leave the cat alone, yet he persists in teasing the cat. Then, one day, the dog begins

DON'T STRESS ME OUT

Your dog doesn't have to deal with paying the bills, the daily commute, PTA meetings and the like, but, believe it or not, there's a lot of stress in a dog's world. Stress can be caused by the owner's impatient demeanor and his angry or harsh corrections. If your dog cringes when you reach for his training collar, he's stressed. An older dog is sometimes stressed out when he goes to a new home. No matter what the cause, put off all training until he's over it. If he's going through a fear period—shying away from people, trembling when spoken to, avoiding eye contact or hiding under furniture—wait to resume training. Naturally you'd also postpone your lessons if the dog were sick, and the same goes for you. Show some compassion.

chasing the cat but the cat turns and takes a swipe at the dog, leaving the dog with a painful gash on his nose. The final result is that the dog stops chasing the cat. Again, a behavior that results in an unpleasant event tends not to be repeated. In training a dog, a sharp "No" is sufficient; never physically punish your dog.

TRAINING EQUIPMENT

COLLAR AND LEASH

For a Kelpie, the collar and leash that you use for training must be one with which you are easily able to work, not too heavy for the dog and perfectly safe.

TREATS

Have a bag of treats on hand; something nutritious and easy to swallow works best. Use a soft

Treats also can be used as motivators. This pup is coaxed to come to his owner with promise of a tasty reward.

treat, a chunk of cheese or a piece of grilled chicken rather than a dry biscuit. By the time the dog has finished chewing a dry treat, he will forget why he is being rewarded in the first place!

Using food rewards will not teach a dog to beg at the table—the only way to teach a dog to beg at the table is to give him food from the table. In training, rewarding the dog with a food treat will help him associate praise and the treats with learning new behaviors that obviously please you.

TRAINING BEGINS: ASK THE DOG A QUESTION

In order to teach your dog anything, you must first get his attention. After all, he cannot learn anything if he is looking away from you with his mind on something else. To get your dog's attention, ask him "School?" and immediately walk over to him and give him a treat as you tell him "Good dog." Wait a minute or two and repeat the routine, this time with a treat in your hand as you approach within a foot of the dog. Do not go directly to him, but stop about a foot short of him and hold out the treat as you ask "School?" He will see you approaching with a treat in your hand and most likely begin walking toward you. As you meet, give him the treat and praise again.

The third time, ask the question, have a treat in your hand and walk only a short distance toward the dog so that he must walk almost all the way to you. As he reaches you, give him the treat and praise again. By this time, the dog will probably be getting the idea that if he pays attention to you, especially when you ask that question, it will pay off in treats and enjoyable activities for him. In other words, he learns that "School" means doing great things with you that are fun and that result in positive attention for him.

Remember that the dog does not understand your verbal language; he only recognizes sounds. Your question translates to a series of sounds for him, and those sounds become the signal to

SMILE WHEN YOU ORDER ME AROUND!

While trainers recommend practicing with your dog every day, it's perfectly acceptable to take a "mental health day" off. It's better not to train the dog on days when you're in a sour mood. Your bad attitude or lack of interest will be sensed by your dog, and he will respond accordingly. Studies show that dogs are well tuned in to their humans' emotions. Be conscious of how you use your voice when talking to your dog. Raising your voice or shouting will only erode your dog's trust in you as his trainer and master.

go to you and pay attention. The dog learns that if he does this, he will get to interact with you plus receive treats and praise.

THE BASIC COMMANDS

TEACHING SIT

Now that you have the dog's attention, attach his leash and hold it in your left hand, and hold a food treat in your right hand. Place your food hand at the dog's nose and let him lick the treat but not take it from you. Say "Sit" and slowly raise your food hand from in front of the dog's nose up over his head so that he is looking at the ceiling. As he bends his head upward, he will have to bend his knees to maintain his balance. As he bends his knees, he will assume a sit position. At that point, release the food treat and

READY, SIT, GO!

On your marks, get set: train! Most professional trainers agree that the sit command is the place to start your dog's formal education. Sitting is a natural posture for most dogs, and they respond to the sit exercise willingly and readily. For every lesson, begin with the sit command so that you start out on a successful note; likewise, you should practice the sit command at the end of every lesson as well, because you always want to end on a high note.

praise lavishly with comments such as "Good dog! Good sit!" Remember to always praise enthusiastically, because dogs relish verbal praise from their owners and feel so proud of themselves whenever they accomplish a behavior.

You will not use food forever in getting the dog to obey your commands. Food is only used to teach new behaviors and, once the dog knows what you want when you give a specific command, you will wean him off the food treats but still maintain the verbal praise. After all, you will always have your voice with you, and there will be many times when you have no food rewards but expect the dog to obey.

You must build a bond with your independent-thinking Kelpie so he understands that you are the leader, not the other way around.

TEACHING DOWN

Teaching the down exercise is easy when you understand how the dog perceives the down position, and it is very difficult when you do not. Dogs perceive the down position as a submissive one; therefore, teaching the down exercise by using a forceful method can sometimes make the dog develop such a fear of the down that he either runs away when you say "Down" or he attempts to snap at the person who tries to force him down.

SIT AROUND THE HOUSE

"Sit" is the command you'll use most often. Your pup objects when placed in a sit with your hands, so try the "bringing the food up under his chin" method. Better still, catch him in the act! Your dog will sit on his own many times throughout the day, so let him know that he's doing the "Sit" by rewarding him. Praise him and have him sit for everything—toys, connecting his leash, his dinner, before going out the door, etc.

Some gentle guidance can be used to ease the dog into the sit position as he gets the hang of it.

Have the dog sit close alongside your left leg, facing in the same direction as you are. Hold the leash in your left hand and a food treat in your right. Now place your left hand lightly on the top of the dog's shoulders where they meet above the spinal cord. Do not push down on the dog's shoulders; simply rest your left hand there so you can guide the dog to lie down close to your left leg rather than to swing away from your side when he drops.

Now place the food hand at the dog's nose, say "Down" very softly (almost a whisper) and slowly lower the food hand to the dog's front feet. When the food hand reaches the floor, begin moving it forward along the floor in front of the dog. Keep talking softly to the dog, saying things like, "Do you want this treat? You can do this, good dog." Your reassuring tone of voice will help calm the dog as he tries to follow the food hand in order to get the treat.

When the dog's elbows touch the floor, release the food and praise softly. Try to get the dog to maintain that down position for several seconds before you let him sit up again. The goal here is to get the dog to settle down and not feel threatened in the down position.

TEACHING STAY

It is easy to teach the dog to stay in either a sit or a down position. Again, we use food and praise during the teaching process as we help the dog to understand exactly what it is that we are expecting him to do.

To teach the sit/stay, start with the dog sitting on your left side as before and hold the leash in your left hand. Have a food treat in

Once your Kelpie is comfortable in the down position, you can begin the down/stay. Give the verbal and hand signal before you step away from your dog.

OKAY!

This is the signal that tells your dog that he can quit whatever he was doing. Use "Okay" to end a session on a correct response to a command. (Never end on an incorrect response.) Lots of praise follows. People use "Okay" a lot and it has other uses for dogs, too. Your dog is barking. You say, "Okay! Come!" "Okay" signals him to stop the barking activity and "Come" allows him to come to you for a "Good dog."

your right hand and place your food hand at the dog's nose. Say "Stay" and step out on your right foot to stand directly in front of the dog, toe to toe, as he licks and nibbles the treat. Be sure to keep his head facing upward to maintain the sit position. Count to five and then swing around to stand next to the dog again with him on your left. As soon as you get back to the original position, release the food and praise lavishly.

To teach the down/stay, do the down as previously described. As soon as the dog lies down, say "Stay" and step out on your right foot just as you did in the sit/stay.

This is how you want your Kelpie to be during training: alert, focused on you and ready for your next instruction.

facing the dog as a stay signal, much the same as the hand signal a police officer uses to stop traffic at an intersection. Hold the food treat in your right hand as before, but this time the food will not be touching the dog's nose. He will watch the food hand and quickly learn that he is going to get that treat as soon as you return to his side.

When you can stand 3 feet away from your dog for 30 seconds, you can then begin building time and distance in both stays. Eventually, the dog can be expected to remain in the stay position for prolonged periods of time until you return to him or call him to you. Always praise lavishly when he stays.

TEACHING COME
If you make teaching the come exercise a fun experience, you should never have a student that

Count to five and then return to stand beside the dog with him on your left side. Release the treat and praise as always.

Within a week or ten days, you can begin to add a bit of distance between you and your dog when you leave him. Start off with the dog on a long training leash, and only progress to practicing to off leash in a securely enclosed area. When you move away from the dog and give the verbal command, also use your left hand held up with the palm

KEEP IT SIMPLE—AND FUN
Keep your lessons simple, interesting and user-friendly. Fun breaks help you both. Spend two minutes or ten teaching your puppy, but practice only as long as your dog enjoys what he's doing and is focused on pleasing you. If he's bored or distracted, stop the training session after any correct response (always end on a high note!). After a few minutes of playtime, you can go back to "hitting the books."

called, the owner is likely to be upset or anxious and he allows these feelings to come through in the tone of his voice when he calls his dog. Hearing that desperation in his owner's voice, the dog fears the results of going to his owner and therefore either disobeys outright or runs in the opposite direction. The secret, therefore, is to teach the dog a game and, when you want him to come to you, simply play the game. Many have found success with this method.

To begin, have several members of your family take a few food treats and each go into a different room in the house. Everyone takes turns calling the dog with "Where are you?" and each person should celebrate the dog's finding him with a treat and lots of happy praise. When a

does not love the game or that fails to come when called. The secret, it seems, is not to teach the word "Come."

At times when an owner most wants his dog to come when

As you progress with the stay command, you will increase both your distance from the dog and the time for which he is expected to stay.

Use a cheerful tone of voice and arms outstretched to call your dog to come to you.

person calls the dog, he is actually inviting the dog to find him and to get a treat as a reward for "winning."

A few turns of the "Where are you?" game and the dog will understand that everyone is playing the game and that each person has a big celebration awaiting the dog's success at locating him or her. Once the dog learns to love the game, simply calling out "Where are you?" will bring him running from wherever he is when he hears that all-important question.

The come command is recognized as one of the most important things to teach a dog, but there are trainers who work with thousands of dogs and never use the actual word "Come." Yet these dogs will race to respond to a person who uses the dog's name followed by "Where are you?" For example, a woman has a 12-year-old companion dog who went blind, but who never fails to locate her owner when asked, "Where are you?"

Children, in particular, love to play this game with their dogs. Children can hide in smaller places like a shower stall or bathtub, behind a bed or under a table. The dog needs to work a

COME AND GET IT!

The come command is your dog's safety signal. Until he is 99% perfect in responding, don't use the come command if you cannot enforce it. Practice on leash with treats or squeakers, or whenever the dog is running to you. Never call him to come to you if he is to be corrected for a misdemeanor. Reward the dog with a treat and happy praise whenever he comes to you.

LET'S GO!

Many people use "Let's go" instead of "Heel" when teaching their dogs to behave on lead. It sounds more like fun! When beginning to teach the heel, whatever command you use, always step off on your left foot. That's the one next to the dog, who is on your left side, in case you've forgotten. Keep a loose leash. When the dog pulls ahead, stop, bring him back and begin again. Use treats to guide him around turns.

little bit harder to find these hiding places, but, when he does, he loves to celebrate with a treat and a tussle with a favorite youngster.

TEACHING HEEL

In obedience circles, heeling means that the dog walks beside the owner without pulling; of course, heeling for a stockdog is completely different matter when it comes to moving cattle. Here we are discussing obedience heeling, which takes time and patience on the owner's part. The goal is to teach the dog that you will not proceed unless the dog is walking calmly beside you. Neither pulling out ahead on the leash nor lagging behind is acceptable.

Begin by holding the leash in your left hand as the dog sits beside your left leg. Move the loop end of the leash to your right hand, but keep your left hand short on the leash so that it keeps the dog in close next to you.

Say "Heel" and step forward on your left foot. Keep the dog close to you and take three steps. Stop and have the dog sit next to you in what we now call the heel position. Praise verbally, but do not touch the dog. Hesitate a moment and begin again with "Heel," taking three steps and stopping, at which point the dog is told to sit again. Your goal here is to have the dog walk those three steps without pulling on the leash. Once he will walk calmly beside you for three steps without pulling, increase the number of steps you take to five. When he

Heeling means that you set the pace of your walk and your dog follows suit, staying at your side.

will walk politely beside you while you take five steps, you can increase the length of your walk to ten steps. Keep increasing the length of your stroll until the dog will walk quietly beside you without pulling as long as you want him to heel. When you stop heeling, indicate to the dog that the exercise is over by verbally praising as you pet him and say "OK, good dog." The "OK" is used as a release word, meaning that the exercise is finished and the dog is free to relax.

If you are dealing with a dog who insists on pulling you around, simply "put on your brakes" and stand your ground

MORE PRAISE, LESS FOOD
As you progress with your puppy's lessons, and the puppy is responding well, gradually begin to wean him off the treats by alternating the treats with times when you offer only verbal praise or a few pats on the dog's side. (Pats on the head are dominant actions, so he won't think they are meant to be praise.) Every lesson should end with the puppy's performing the correct action for that session's command. When he gets it right and you withhold the treat, the praise can be as long and lavish as you like. The commands are one word only, but your verbal praise can use as many words as you want...don't skimp!

This future trainer is proud of her star student, demonstrating a nice sit.

until the dog realizes that the two of you are not going anywhere until he is beside you and moving at your pace, not his. It may take some time just standing there to convince the dog that you are the leader and that you will be the one to decide on the direction and speed of your travel.

Each time the dog looks up at you or slows down to give a slack leash between the two of you, quietly praise him and say, "Good heel. Good dog." Eventually, the dog will begin to respond and within a few days he should be walking politely beside you without pulling on the leash. At first, the training sessions should be kept short; soon the dog will be able to walk nicely with you for increasingly longer distances. Always keep things very positive, and remember also to give the dog free time and the opportunity to run and play when you have finished heel practice.

TRAINING THE KELPIE PUPPY FOR HERDING

Kelpie puppies usually start showing the initiative to herd when they are about eight weeks of age. This can vary depending on the line, with some puppies

When a dog is well behaved on leash, walking him is enjoyable for both dog and owner.

TIPS FOR TRAINING AND SAFETY

1. Whether on or off leash, practice only in a fenced area.
2. Remove the training collar when the training session is over.
3. Don't try to break up a dogfight.
4. "Come," "Leave it" and "Wait" are safety commands.
5. The dog belongs in a crate or behind a barrier when riding in the car.
6. Don't ignore the dog's first sign of aggression. Aggression only gets worse, so take it seriously.
7. Keep the faces of children and dogs separated.
8. Pay attention to what the dog is chewing.
9. Keep the vet's number near your phone.
10. "Okay" is a useful release command.

beginning as late as four or five months old. If you have acquired a working puppy, then you want to build up your puppy's confidence in every little task he does. You want to convince him that he's "Superkelpie," the unstoppable herding dog! While socializing the puppy to the livestock, introduce the pup to some of the commands that you will use in working, which are different from the basic obedience commands. For an eight-week-old Kelpie, you would select a younger or milder sheep rather than an unruly bull. What's important is that the Kelpie gets used to the smell, sound and look of the stock and that he is never frightened or injured. Keep training experiences positive and praise your puppy every step of the way.

A well-bred working Kelpie has the ideal calm temperament and trains easily to the livestock. Some puppies show a natural tendency to block the sheep and to move them towards the handler. Again, this varies depending on the dogs and the line. When the puppy shows signs that he wants to "move" the sheep or ducks, let him. Assist him quietly by moving the herd or flock, all the while letting the puppy think he's "the boss." It's all about the puppy's mindset and his confidence. Be mindful that your Kelpie kid doesn't become frustrated or too worn out. A puppy is not built to run up and down hills for hours at a time.

In order to properly train your stockdog, you will need to work directly with a professional herdsperson and the livestock. You have to get to know the livestock and, of course, the dog. No dog, no matter how talented or well bred, learns the ropes overnight. It's a matter of patience,

The Kelpie is more often seen on the farm than in conformation shows, but the breed does cut a striking presence in the ring.

and few of them have a yard full of cows! That said, let's discuss what it requires to keep a Kelpie as a sane and happy pet.

Kelpie owners do not have the option of offering their dogs a passive existence. While some Kelpies may survive a life as a house and backyard dog with several walks a day, most will go stir-crazy given such a lifestyle. Kelpies, like their active, go-get-'em owners, have similar emotions, drives and needs.

Dogs can become so frustrated and bored they begin to exhibit extremely undesirable behavior such as chewing up furniture, woodwork, clothing, etc. They will bark incessantly for no apparent reason (it's caused by frustration!). They

praise and persistence, the same recipe for success in all matters of dog training.

ACTIVITIES FOR YOUR KELPIE AND YOU

Let's begin by saying that the Kelpie was born and bred for a singular purpose: stockdog work. Most breeders concur that there is no substitute for real yard work on cattle and sheep. No one could contest that there's any viable way to keep a Kelpie who is accustomed to working for eight non-stop hours on cattle busy all day. Not even if you dressed your Kelpie up and sent him off to Wall Street would your cattle dog feel happy and productive. Due to the breed's many positive characteristics, his natural good looks and his intelligence, many people are attracted to this Australian wonder

A well-trained Kelpie behaving nicely on lead for his young walking partner.

sometimes void in inappropriate places such as in the house, on a porch, around a pool or on the owner's bed.

Before long, the dog is so out of control the owner decides he can't cope with the problem behavior anymore. He turns the dog over to an animal shelter. If the dog is lucky, he'll be rehomed by someone who really cares and is willing to work with the dog to develop a new and better lifestyle. If he's not lucky, he faces euthanasia. Therein lies the tragedy of the neglected pet dog.

In your search for just the right dog for you, make plans right from the start to get active with your dog. In the case of Kelpies, keeping active is not a choice, it's a *must*! The dog will love doing things with you. You'll enjoy the excitement and pleasure of having a new hobby that includes your canine friend. What can we do together, you ask? The list of activity possibilities is almost endless. Actually, it's limited only by your own imagination and willingness to join your dog in exciting activities.

KELPIE TESTS AND TRIALS
Tests and trials for Kelpies are given by breed and stockdog clubs that offer yard trials, utility trials and arena trials. Some of these

In competitive herding events, a course is set up to simulate a working scenario and the dog's performace is evaluated.

activities use sheep; others employ ducks because ducks naturally stick together in a flock, making it easier for the dog to herd them from one place to another. In addition, herding ducks is less intimidating for beginner dogs than facing large stubborn sheep that seem to say, "Make me!" Most Kelpies, however, aren't intimidated by anything covered in wool.

Herding tests provide the opportunity for Kelpies to earn herding titles. Trials offer competition among the Kelpies to show how good they are at herding. From the trials, dogs can earn even more sophisticated titles that designate their herding proficiency. All-breed herding clubs, stockdog associations and some obedience clubs sponsor these tests and trials. You can get specific information about the sponsoring organizations and types of activities through your breeder or by contacting the organization with which your Kelpie is registered.

ACTIVITIES FOR ALL BREEDS

All-breed activities are broken down into two groups: individual activities and team activities. These activities are open to all owners and their dogs, pure-bred and mixed. If an owner lives too far away from a club that runs team

With a lot of instinct and a little guidance, the Kelpie takes naturally to moving the flock.

There's no mistaking the body language of a dog who is looking for a place to "go."

There's no mistaking the body language of a dog who is looking for a place to "go."

activities, the owner can still work with his dog in solo activities. For example, many years ago I had a dog named Royal who was just begging for something to do. I taught her to backpack and we'd set out in a nearby park just as dawn broke on several mornings a week. We'd backpack wooded trails, stop halfway and rest as we watched the birds begin their day. The backpack she wore contained a large dog biscuit for her and a few sweet biscuits for me. I carried water in a container over my shoulder and we always enjoyed a cool drink.

By the time we got back home, Royal was ready for a nap and I was ready for a shower and my day on the job. This routine lasted for several years, giving Royal a purpose and a rewarding activity to share with me while I relished the pleasure of her company in a healthy endeavor.

Other individual activities include jogging, camping, swimming, helping around the yard and Frisbee®. Of course, there are always trick training and playing fetch, which every dog can learn for fun and an occasional food reward.

Tracking is an activity that can be done by any breed of dog. It can also be done by mixed-breed dogs although they are not able to earn titles. The activity itself teaches a dog to follow the path of a person who has gone ahead of him minutes or hours before. Tracking can be taught individually by the owner, providing he has a good book on how to teach the dog to track or someone to advise him. It's also helpful if the owner/dog team has someone who is willing to lay the track for them to follow. Obedience schools might offer classes to help to get started, or you may find a local dog club with tracking enthusiasts. It's an extremely rewarding activity that provides lots of healthy exercise for dog and owner.

Team activities such as agility and obedience trials, flyball and rally obedience require appropriate equipment and available locations. Because they include many people and dogs, they are usually exciting, noisy, hectic and lots of fun. In addition, they're usually

conducted on a preplanned schedule. In certain events, dogs of different breeds compete against each other, usually in groups divided by size. For example, there may be separate categories for toy, small, medium and large dogs, divided by height specifications.

When you see an announcement for an event or trial in your area, take advantage of it and go to observe. At an obedience competition, for example, you will see classes from basic control (Novice level) to very advanced control (Utility level) activities. Chances are you'll be impressed by the dogs' accomplishments in demonstrating their ability to work with their owners and perform commands such as heeling, staying, fetching (retrieving) and jumping (the last

Taking a breather is a handsome group of Kelpies owned by Roger Urricelquis.

one being an advanced activity). After watching obedience classes, you may decide that you and your dog should join the sport, too.

There are many sources of information about getting involved in dog activities, such as the national registries and breed clubs, local breed clubs, dog obedience clubs and schools, books, magazines, local fairs and your local newspaper. The national organizations are usually the ones that sponsor sanctioned events and award titles of achievement.

Kelpies are extremely intelli-gent and eager to please. These qualities make them ideal candidates for many dog activi-ties. They love learning and going places with their owners. They are not usually people- or dog-aggressive, so they do well in situations with other dogs and owners. They adapt well to various situations, so introducing them to new activities is easy. They're quick learners and rarely need too much instruction to get the hang of a new sport or activity. In short, Kelpies love keeping busy, so sharing an active lifestyle with them is precisely what they need.

HEALTHCARE OF YOUR

AUSTRALIAN KELPIE

By Lowell Ackerman DVM, DACVD

HEALTHCARE FOR A LIFETIME
When you own a dog, you become his healthcare advocate over his entire lifespan, as well as being the one to shoulder the financial burden of such care. Accordingly, it is worthwhile to focus on prevention rather than treatment, as you and your pet will both be happier.

Of course, the best place to have begun your program of preventive healthcare is with the initial purchase or adoption of your dog. You certainly should have done adequate research into the Australian Kelpie and have selected your puppy carefully rather than buying on impulse. Health issues aside, a large number of pet abandonment and relinquishment cases arise from a mismatch between pet needs and owner expectations. This is entirely preventable with appropriate planning and finding a good breeder.

Regarding healthcare issues specifically, it is very difficult to make blanket statements about where to acquire a problem-free pet, but, again, a reputable breeder is your best bet. In an ideal situation you have the opportunity to see both parents, get references from other owners of the breeder's pups and see genetic-testing documentation for several generations of the litter's ancestors. At the very least, you must thoroughly investigate the Australian Kelpie and the problems inherent in that breed, as well as the genetic testing available to screen for those problems. Genetic testing offers some important benefits, but is available for only a few disorders in a relatively small number of breeds and is not available for some of the most common genetic diseases, such as hip dysplasia, cataracts, epilepsy, cardiomyopathy, etc. This area of research is indeed exciting and increasingly important, and advances will continue to be made each year. In fact, recent research has shown that there is an equivalent dog gene for 75% of known human genes, so research done in either species is likely to benefit the other.

We've also discussed that evaluating the behavioral nature of your Australian Kelpie and that of

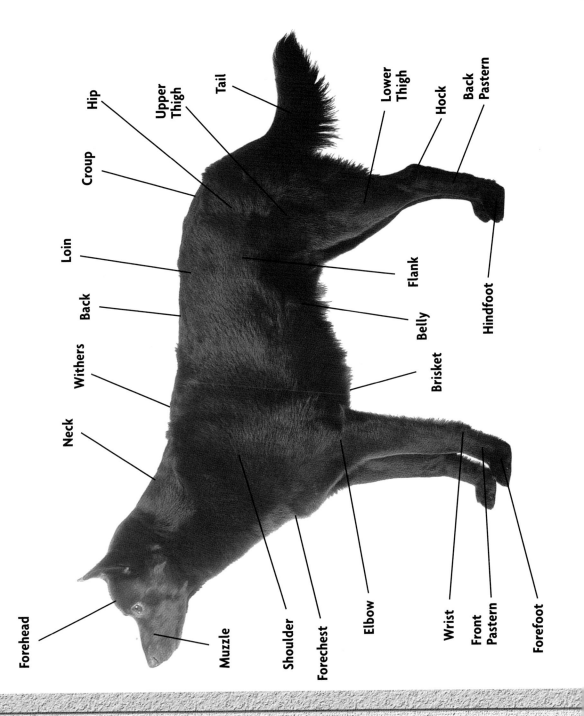

Forehead

Muzzle

Neck

Withers

Back

Loin

Croup

Hip

Upper Thigh

Tail

Lower Thigh

Hock

Back Pastern

Flank

Hindfoot

Belly

Brisket

Shoulder

Forechest

Elbow

Wrist

Front Pastern

Forefoot

PHYSICAL STRUCTURE OF THE AUSTRALIAN KELPIE

his immediate family members is an important part of the selection process that cannot be overemphasized. It is sometimes difficult to evaluate temperament in puppies because certain behavioral tendencies, such as some forms of aggression, may not be immediately evident. More dogs are euthanized each year for behavioral reasons than for all medical conditions combined, so it is critical to take temperament issues seriously. Start with a well-balanced, friendly companion and put the time and effort into proper socialization.

Assuming that you have started off with a pup from healthy, sound stock, you then become responsible for helping your veterinarian keep your pet healthy. Parasite control typically begins with the breeder at two weeks of age, and vaccinations typically begin at six to eight weeks of age. A pre-pubertal evaluation is typically scheduled for about six months of age. At this time, a dental evaluation is done (since the adult teeth are now in), heartworm prevention is started and neutering or spaying is most commonly done.

It is critical to commence regular dental care at home if you have not already done so. It may not sound very important, but most dogs have active periodontal disease by four years of age if they don't have their teeth cleaned regularly at home, not just at their

veterinary exams. Dental problems lead to more than just bad "doggy breath." Gum disease can have very serious medical consequences. If you start brushing your dog's teeth and using antiseptic rinses from a young age, your dog will be accustomed to it and will not resist. The results will be healthy dentition, which your pet will need to enjoy a long, healthy life.

Even individual dogs within each breed have different healthcare requirements, so work with your veterinarian to determine what will be needed and what your role should be. This doctor-client relationship is important, because as vaccination guidelines change, there may not be an annual "vaccine visit" scheduled. You must make sure that you see your veterinarian at least annually, even if no vaccines are due, because this is the best opportunity to coordinate healthcare activities and to make sure that no medical issues creep by unaddressed.

When your Australian Kelpie reaches three-quarters of his anticipated lifespan, he is considered a "senior" and likely requires some special care. In general, if you've been taking great care of your canine companion throughout his formative and adult years, the transition to senior status should be a smooth one. Age is not a disease, and as long as everything is functioning as it should, there is

1. Esophagus
2. Lungs
3. Spleen
4. Liver
5. Stomach
6. Intestines
7. Urinary Bladder

INTERNAL ORGANS OF THE AUSTRALIAN KELPIE

no reason why most of late adulthood should not be rewarding for both you and your pet. This is especially true if you have tended to the details, such as regular veterinary visits, proper dental care, excellent nutrition and management of bone and joint issues. At this stage in your Australian Kelpie's life, your veterinarian may want to schedule visits twice yearly, and make some adjustments to your Kelpie's everyday care, such as his diet. Catching problems early is the best way to manage them effectively.

SELECTING A VETERINARIAN

There is probably no more important decision that you will make regarding your pet's health-care than the selection of his doctor. Your pet's veterinarian will be a pediatrician, family-practice physician and gerontologist, depending on the dog's life stage, and will be the individual who makes recommendations regarding issues such as when specialists need to be consulted, when diagnostic testing and/or therapeutic intervention is needed and when you will need to seek outside emergency and critical-care services. Your vet will act as your advocate and liaison throughout these processes.

Everyone has his own idea about what to look for in a vet, an individual who will play a big role in his dog's (and, of course, his own) life for many years to come. For some, it is the compassionate caregiver with whom they hope to develop a professional relationship to span the lives of their dogs and even their future pets. For others, they are seeking a clinician with keen diagnostic and therapeutic insight who can deliver state-of-the-art healthcare. Still others need a veterinary facility that is open evenings and weekends, is in close proximity or provides mobile veterinary services to accommodate their schedules; these people may not much mind that their dogs might see different veterinarians on each visit. Just as we have different reasons for selecting our own healthcare professionals (e.g., covered by insurance plan, expert in field, convenient location, etc.), we should not expect that there is a one-size-fits-all recommendation for selecting a veterinarian and veterinary practice. The best advice is to be honest in your assessment of what you expect from a veterinary practice and to conscientiously research the options in your area. You will quickly appreciate that not all veterinary practices are the same, and you will be happiest with one that truly meets your needs.

There is another point to be considered in the selection of veterinary services. Not that long ago, a single veterinarian would attempt to manage all medical and surgical issues as they arose. That

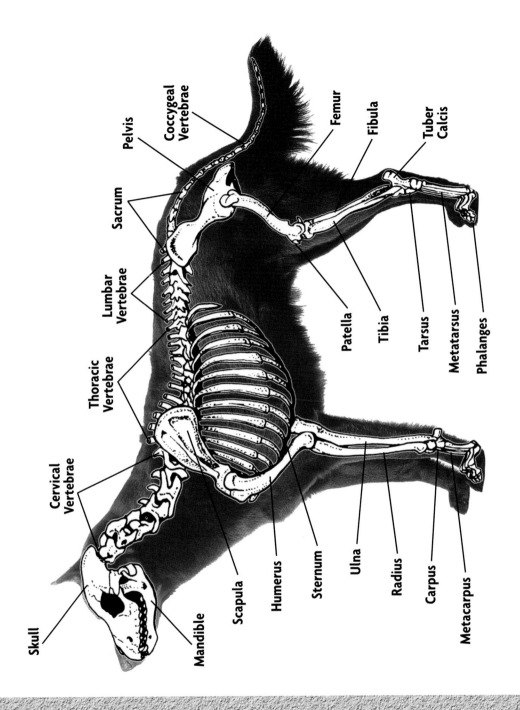

Coccygeal Vertebrae
Pelvis
Sacrum
Femur
Fibula
Tuber Calcis
Lumbar Vertebrae
Thoracic Vertebrae
Cervical Vertebrae
Patella
Tibia
Tarsus
Metatarsus
Phalanges
Skull
Mandible
Scapula
Humerus
Sternum
Ulna
Radius
Carpus
Metacarpus

SKELETAL STRUCTURE OF THE AUSTRALIAN KELPIE

was often problematic, because veterinarians are trained in many species and many diseases, and it was just impossible for general veterinary practitioners to be experts in every species, every breed, every field and every ailment. However, just as in the human healthcare fields, specialization has allowed general practitioners to concentrate on primary healthcare delivery, especially wellness and the prevention of infectious diseases, and to utilize a network of specialists to assist in the management of conditions that require specific expertise and experience. Thus there are now many types of veterinary specialists, including dermatologists, cardiologists, ophthalmologists, surgeons, internists, oncologists, neurologists, behaviorists, criticalists and others to help primary-care veterinarians deal with complicated medical challenges. In most cases, specialists see cases referred by primary-care veterinarians, make diagnoses and set up management plans. From there, the animals' ongoing care is returned to their primary-care veterinarians. This important team approach to your pet's medical-care needs has provided opportunities for advanced care and an unparalleled level of quality to be delivered.

With all of the opportunities for your Australian Kelpie to receive high-quality veterinary medical care, there is another topic

that needs to be addressed at the same time—cost. It's been said that you can have excellent healthcare

YOUR DOG NEEDS TO VISIT THE VET IF:
• He has ingested a toxin such as antifreeze or a toxic plant; in these cases, administer first aid and call the vet right away
• His teeth are discolored, loose or missing or he has sores or other signs of infection or abnormality in the mouth
• He has been vomiting, has had diarrhea or has been constipated for over 24 hours; call immediately if you notice blood
• He has refused food for over 24 hours
• His eating habits, water intake or toilet habits have noticeably changed; if you have noticed weight gain or weight loss
• He shows symptoms of bloat, which requires *immediate* attention
• He is salivating excessively
• He has a lump in his throat
• He has a lump or bumps anywhere on the body
• He is very lethargic
• He appears to be in pain or otherwise has trouble chewing or swallowing
• His skin loses elasticity.
    Of course, there will be other instances in which a visit to the vet is necessary; these are just some of the signs that could be indicative of serious problems that need to be caught as early as possible.

or inexpensive healthcare, but never both; this is as true in veterinary medicine as it is in human medicine. While veterinary costs are a fraction of what the same services cost in the human healthcare arena, it is still difficult to deal with unanticipated medical costs, especially since they can easily creep into hundreds or even thousands of dollars if specialists or emergency services become involved. However, there are ways of managing these risks. The easiest is to buy pet health insurance and realize that its foremost purpose is not to cover routine healthcare visits but rather to serve as an umbrella for those rainy days when your pet needs medical care and you don't want to worry about whether or not you can afford that care.

Pet insurance policies are very cost-effective (and very inexpensive by human health-insurance standards), but make sure that you buy the policy long before you intend to use it (preferably starting in puppyhood, because coverage will exclude pre-existing conditions) and that you are actually buying an indemnity insurance plan from an insurance company that is regulated by your state or province. Many insurance policy look-alikes are actually discount clubs that are redeemable only at specific locations and for specific services. An indemnity plan covers your pet at almost all veterinary, specialty and emergency practices and is an excellent way to manage your pet's ongoing healthcare needs.

VACCINATIONS AND INFECTIOUS DISEASES

There has never been an easier time to prevent a variety of infectious diseases in your dog, but the advances we've made in veterinary medicine come with a price—choice. Now while it may seem that this choice is a good thing (and it is), it also has never been more difficult for the pet owner (or the veterinarian) to make an informed decision about the best way to protect pets through vaccination.

Years ago, it was just accepted that puppies got a starter series of vaccinations and then annual "boosters" throughout their lives to keep them protected. As more and more vaccines became available, consumers wanted the convenience of having all of that protection in a single injection. The result was "multivalent" vaccines that crammed a lot of protection into a single syringe. The manufacturers' recommendations were to give the vaccines annually, and this was a simple enough protocol to follow. However, as veterinary medicine has become more sophisticated and we have started looking more at healthcare quandaries rather than convenience, it became necessary to reevaluate the situation and deal

COMMON INFECTIOUS DISEASES

Let's discuss some of the diseases that create the need for vaccination in the first place. Following are the major canine infectious diseases and a simple explanation of each.

Rabies: A devastating viral disease that can be fatal in dogs and people. In fact, vaccination of dogs and cats is an important public-health measure to create a resistant animal buffer population to protect people from contracting the disease. Vaccination schedules are determined on a government level and are not optional for pet owners; rabies vaccination is required by law in all 50 states.

Parvovirus: A severe, potentially life-threatening disease that is easily transmitted between dogs. There are four strains of the virus, but it is believed that there is significant "cross-protection" between strains that may be included in individual vaccines.

Distemper: A potentially severe and life-threatening disease with a relatively high risk of exposure, especially in certain regions. In very high-risk distemper environments, young pups may be vaccinated with human measles vaccine, a related virus that offers cross-protection when administered at four to ten weeks of age.

Hepatitis: Caused by canine adenovirus type 1 (CAV-1), but since vaccination with the causative virus has a higher rate of adverse effects, cross-protection is derived from the use of adenovirus type 2 (CAV-2), a cause of respiratory disease and one of the potential causes of canine cough. Vaccination with CAV-2 provides long-term immunity against hepatitis, but relatively less protection against respiratory infection.

Canine cough: Also called tracheobronchitis, actually a fairly complicated result of viral and bacterial offenders; therefore, even with vaccination, protection is incomplete. Wherever dogs congregate, canine cough will likely be spread among them. Intranasal vaccination with *Bordetella* and parainfluenza is the best safeguard, but the duration of immunity does not appear to be very long, typically a year at most. These are non-core vaccines, but vaccination is sometimes mandated by boarding kennels, obedience classes, dog shows and other places where dogs congregate to try to minimize spread of infection.

Leptospirosis: A potentially fatal disease that is more common in some geographic regions. It is capable of being spread to humans. The disease varies with the individual "serovar," or strain, of *Leptospira* involved. Since there does not appear to be much cross-protection between serovars, protection is only as good as the likelihood that the serovar in the vaccine is the same as the one in the pet's local environment. Problems with *Leptospira* vaccines are that protection does not last very long, side effects are not uncommon and a large percentage of dogs (perhaps 30%) may not respond to vaccination.

Borrelia burgdorferi: The cause of Lyme disease, the risk of which varies with the geographic area in which the pet lives and travels. Lyme disease is spread by deer ticks in the eastern US and western black-legged ticks in the western part of the country, and the risk of exposure is high in some regions. Lameness, fever and inappetence are most commonly seen in affected dogs. The extent of protection from the vaccine has not been conclusively demonstrated.

Coronavirus: This disease has a high risk of exposure, especially in areas where dogs congregate, but it typically causes only mild to moderate digestive upset (diarrhea, vomiting, etc.). Vaccines are available, but the duration of protection is believed to be relatively short and the effectiveness of the vaccine in preventing infection is considered low.

There are many other vaccinations available, including those for *Giardia* and canine adenovirus-1. While there may be some specific indications for their use, and local risk factors to be considered, they are not widely recommended for most dogs.

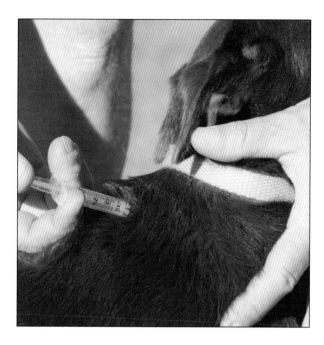

NEUTERING/SPAYING

Sterilization procedures (neutering for males/spaying for females) are meant to accomplish several purposes. While the underlying premise is to address the risk of pet overpopulation, there are also some medical and behavioral benefits to the surgeries as well. For females, spaying prior to the first estrus (heat cycle) leads to a marked reduction in the risk of mammary cancer and other serious female problems. There also will be no manifestations of "heat" to attract male dogs and no bleeding in the house. For males, there is prevention of testicular cancer and a reduction in the risk of prostate problems. In both sexes there may be some limited reduction in aggressive behaviors toward other dogs, and some diminishing of urine marking, roaming and mounting.

While neutering and spaying do indeed prevent animals from contributing to pet overpopulation, even no-cost and low-cost neutering options have not eliminated the problem. Perhaps one of the main reasons for this is that individuals that intentionally breed their dogs and those that allow their animals to run at large are the main causes of unwanted offspring. Also, animals in shelters are often there because they were abandoned or relinquished, not because they came from unplanned matings. Neutering/spaying is

Your Kelpie's vaccination program starts before you bring him home. The breeder will give you all health records so that your vet can continue with the appropriate shots and schedule. with some tough questions. It is important to realize that whether or not to use a particular vaccine depends on the risk of contracting the disease against which it protects, the severity of the disease if it is contracted, the duration of immunity provided by the vaccine, the safety of the product and the needs of the individual animal. In a very general sense, rabies, distemper, hepatitis and parvovirus are considered core vaccine needs, while parainfluenza, *Bordetella bronchiseptica*, leptospirosis, coronavirus and borreliosis (Lyme disease) are considered non-core needs and best reserved for animals that demonstrate reasonable risk of contracting the diseases.

important, but it should be considered in the context of the real causes of animals' ending up in shelters and eventually being euthanized.

One of the important considerations regarding neutering is that it is a surgical procedure. This sometimes gets lost in discussions of low-cost procedures and commoditization of the process. In females, spaying is specifically referred to as an ovariohysterectomy. In this procedure, a midline incision is made in the abdomen and the entire uterus and both ovaries are surgically removed. While this is a major invasive surgical procedure, it usually has few complications, because it is typically performed on healthy young animals. However, it is major surgery, as any woman who has had a hysterectomy will attest.

In males, neutering has traditionally referred to castration, which involves the surgical removal of both testicles. While still a significant piece of surgery, there is not the abdominal exposure that is required in the female surgery. In addition, there is now a chemical sterilization option,

in which a solution is injected into each testicle, leading to atrophy of the sperm-producing cells. This can typically be done under sedation rather than full anesthesia. This is a relatively new approach, and there are no long-term clinical studies yet available.

Neutering/spaying is typically done around six months of age at most veterinary hospitals, although techniques have been pioneered to perform the procedures in animals as young as eight weeks of age. In general, the surgeries on the very young animals are done for the specific reason of sterilizing them before they go to their new homes. This is done in some shelter hospitals for assurance that the animals will definitely not produce any pups. Otherwise, these organizations need to rely on owners to comply with their wishes to have the animals "altered" at a later date, something that does not always happen.

The Kelpie will spend plenty of time outdoors, so check his skin and coat frequently for any signs of problems caused by grasses, pollen, insects or other potential irritants.

S. E. M. BY DR. DENNIS KUNKEL, UNIVERSITY OF HAWAII

A scanning electron micrograph of a dog flea, *Ctenocephalides canis*, on dog hair.

EXTERNAL PARASITES

FLEAS

Fleas have been around for millions of years and, while we have better tools now for controlling them than at any time in the past, there still is little chance that they will end up on an endangered species list. Actually, they are very well adapted to living on our pets, and they continue to adapt as we make advances.

The female flea can consume 15 times her weight in blood during active reproduction and can lay as many as 40 eggs a day. These eggs are very resistant to the effects of insecticides. They hatch into larvae, which then mature and spin cocoons. The immature fleas reside in this pupal stage until the time is right for feeding. This pupal stage is also very resistant to the effects of insecticides, and pupae can last in the environment without feeding for many months. Newly emergent fleas are attracted to animals by the warmth of the animals' bodies, movement and exhaled carbon dioxide. However, when they first emerge from their cocoons, they orient towards light; thus when an animal passes between a flea and the light source, casting a shadow, the flea pounces and starts to feed. If the animal turns out to be a dog or cat, the reproductive cycle continues. If the flea lands on another type of animal, including a person, the flea will bite but will then look for a more appropriate host. An emerging adult flea can survive without feeding for up to 12 months but, once it tastes blood, it can survive off its host for only 3 to 4 days.

It was once thought that fleas spend most of their lives in the environment, but we now know that fleas won't willingly jump off a dog unless leaping to another dog or when physically removed by brushing, bathing or other manipulation. Flea eggs, on the other hand, are shiny and smooth, and they roll off the animal and into the environment. The eggs, larvae and pupae then exist in the environment, but once the adult finds a susceptible animal, it's home sweet home until the flea is forced to seek refuge elsewhere.

Since adult fleas live on the animal and immature forms survive in the environment, a successful treatment plan must address all stages of the flea life cycle. There are now several safe and effective flea-control products that can be applied on a monthly basis. These include fipronil,

FLEA PREVENTION FOR YOUR DOG

- Discuss with your veterinarian the safest product to protect your dog, likely in the form of a monthly tablet or a liquid preparation placed on the back of the dog's neck.
- For dogs suffering from flea-bite dermatitis, a shampoo or topical insecticide treatment is required.
- Your lawn and property should be sprayed with an insecticide designed to kill fleas and ticks that lurk outdoors.
- Using a flea comb, check the dog's coat regularly for any signs of parasites.
- Practice good housekeeping. Vacuum floors, carpets and furniture regularly, especially in the areas that the dog frequents, and wash the dog's bedding weekly.
- Follow up house-cleaning with carpet shampoos and sprays to rid the house of fleas at all stages of development. Insect growth regulators are the safest option.

imidacloprid, selamectin and permethrin (found in several formulations). Most of these products have significant flea-killing rates within 24 hours. However, none of them will control the immature forms in the environment. To accomplish this, there are a variety of insect growth regulators that can be

THE FLEA'S LIFE CYCLE

What came first, the flea or the egg? This age-old mystery is more difficult to comprehend than the

actual cycle of the flea. Fleas usually live only about four months. A female can lay 2,000 eggs in her lifetime.

Egg

After ten days of rolling around your carpet or under your furniture, the eggs hatch into larvae,

Larva

which feed on various and sundry debris. In days or months, depending on the climate, the larvae spin cocoons and develop into the pupal or nymph stage, which quickly develop into fleas.

Pupa

These immature fleas must locate a host within 10 to 14 days or they will die. Only about 1% of the flea population exist as adult fleas, while the other 99% exist as eggs, larvae or pupae.

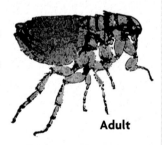

Adult

PHOTO BY CAROLINA BIOLOGICAL SUPPLY CO.

KILL FLEAS THE NATURAL WAY

If you choose not to go the route of conventional medication, there are some natural ways to ward off fleas:

- Dust your dog with a natural flea powder, composed of such herbal goodies as rosemary, wormwood, pennyroyal, citronella, rue, tobacco powder and eucalyptus.
- Apply diatomaceous earth, the fossilized remains of single-cell algae, to your carpets, furniture and pet's bedding. Even though it's not good for dogs, it's even worse for fleas, which will dry up swiftly and die.
- Brush your dog frequently, give him adequate exercise and let him fast occasionally. All of these activities strengthen the dog's immune system and make him more resistant to disease and parasites.
- Bathe your dog with a capful of pennyroyal or eucalyptus oil.
- Feed a natural diet, free of additives and preservatives. Add some fresh garlic and brewer's yeast to the dog's morning portion, as these items have flea-repelling properties.

sprayed into the environment (e.g., pyriproxyfen, methoprene, fenoxycarb) as well as insect development inhibitors such as lufenuron that can be administered. These compounds have no effect on adult fleas, but they stop immature forms from developing into adults. In years gone by, we relied heavily on toxic insecticides (such as organophosphates, organochlorines and carbamates) to manage the flea problem, but today's options are not only much safer to use on our pets but also safer for the environment.

TICKS

Ticks are members of the spider class (arachnids) and are blood-sucking parasites capable of transmitting a variety of diseases, including Lyme disease, ehrlichiosis, babesiosis and Rocky Mountain spotted fever. It's easy to see ticks on your own skin, but it is more of a challenge when your furry companion is affected. Whenever you happen to be planning a stroll in a tick-infested area (especially forests, grassy or wooded areas or parks) be prepared to do a thorough inspection of your dog afterward to search for ticks. Ticks can be tricky, so make sure you spend time looking in the ears, between the toes and everywhere else where a tick might hide. Ticks need to be attached for 24–72 hours before they transmit most of the diseases that they carry, so you do have a window of opportunity for some preventive intervention.

A TICKING BOMB

There is nothing good about a tick's harpooning his nose into your dog's skin. Among the diseases caused by ticks are Rocky Mountain spotted fever, canine ehrlichiosis, canine babesiosis, canine hepatozoonosis and Lyme disease. If a dog is allergic to the saliva of a female wood tick, he can develop tick paralysis.

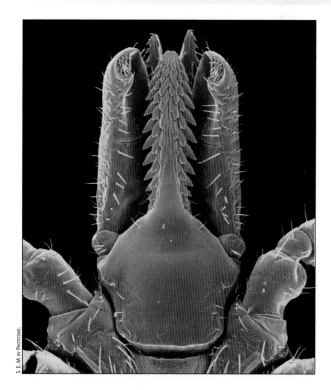

S. E. M. BY PHOTOTAKE.

Female ticks live to eat and breed. They can lay between 4,000 and 5,000 eggs and they die soon after. Males, on the other hand, live only to mate with the females and continue the process as long as they are able. Most ticks live on multiple hosts before parasitizing dogs. The immature forms typically reside on grass and shrubs, waiting for susceptible animals to walk by. The larvae and nymph stages typically feed on wildlife.

If only a few ticks are present on a dog, they can be plucked out, but it is important to remove the entire head and mouthparts,

A scanning electron micrograph of the head of a female deer tick, *Ixodes dammini*, a parasitic tick that carries Lyme disease.

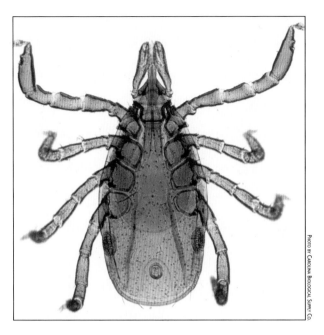

PHOTO BY CAROLINA BIOLOGICAL SUPPLY CO.

Deer tick,
Ixodes dammini.

disposed of in a container of alcohol or household bleach.

Some of the newer flea products, specifically those with fipronil, selamectin and permethrin, have effect against some, but not all, species of tick. Flea collars containing appropriate pesticides (e.g., propoxur, chlorfen-vinphos) can aid in tick control. In most areas, such collars should be placed on animals in March, at the beginning of the tick season, and changed regularly. Leaving the collar on when the pesticide level is waning invites the development of resistance. Amitraz collars are also good for tick control, and the active ingredient does not interfere with other flea-control products. The ingredient helps prevent the attachment of ticks to the skin and will cause those ticks already on the skin to detach themselves.

which may be deeply embedded in the skin. This is best accomplished with forceps designed especially for this purpose; fingers can be used but should be protected with rubber gloves, plastic wrap or at least a paper towel. The tick should be grasped as closely as possible to the animal's skin and should be pulled upward with steady, even pressure. Do not squeeze, crush or puncture the body of the tick or you risk exposure to any disease carried by that tick. Once the ticks have been removed, the sites of attachment should be disinfected. Your hands should then be washed with soap and water to further minimize risk of contagion. The tick should be

TICK CONTROL

Removal of underbrush and leaf litter and the thinning of trees in areas where tick control is desired are recom-mended. These actions remove the cover and food sources for small animals that serve as hosts for ticks. With continued mowing of grasses in these areas, the probability of ticks' surviving is further reduced. A variety of insecticide ingredients (e.g., resmethrin, carbaryl, permethrin, chlorpyrifos, dioxathion and allethrin) are registered for tick control around the home.

Mites

Mites are tiny arachnid parasites that parasitize the skin of dogs. Skin diseases caused by mites are referred to as "mange," and there are many different forms seen in dogs. These forms are very different from one another, each one warranting an individual description.

Sarcoptic mange, or scabies, is one of the itchiest conditions that affects dogs. The microscopic *Sarcoptes* mites burrow into the superficial layers of the skin and can drive dogs crazy with itchiness. They are also communicable to people, although they can't complete their reproductive cycle on people. In addition to being tiny, the mites also are often difficult to find when trying to make a diagnosis. Skin scrapings from multiple areas are examined microscopically but, even then, sometimes the mites cannot be found.

Fortunately, scabies is relatively easy to treat, and there are a variety of products that will successfully kill the mites. Since the mites can't live in the environment for very long without feeding, a complete cure is usually possible within four to eight weeks.

Cheyletiellosis is caused by a relatively large mite, which sometimes can be seen even without a microscope. Often referred to as "walking dandruff," this also causes itching, but not usually as profound as with scabies.

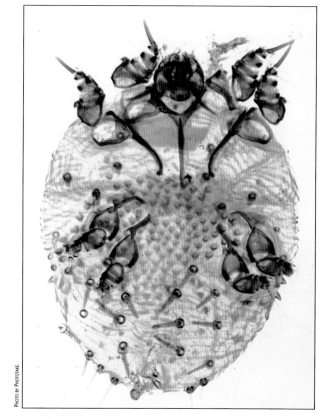

PHOTO BY PHOTOTAKE.

Sarcoptes scabiei, commonly known as the "itch mite."

While *Cheyletiella* mites can survive somewhat longer in the environment than scabies mites, they too are relatively easy to treat, being responsive to not only the medications used to treat scabies but also often to flea-control products.

Otodectes cynotis is the canine ear mite and is one of the more common causes of mange, especially in young dogs in shelters or pet stores. That's because the mites are typically present in large numbers and are quickly spread to

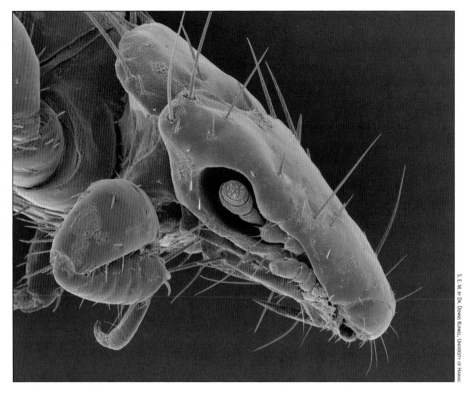

Micrograph of a dog louse, *Heterodoxus spiniger*. Female lice attach their eggs to the hairs of the dog. As the eggs hatch, the larval lice bite and feed on the blood. Lice can also feed on dead skin and hair. This feeding activity can cause hair loss and skin problems.

S. E. M. by Dr. Dennis Kunkel, University of Hawaii

nearby animals. The mites rarely do much harm but can be difficult to eradicate if the treatment regimen is not comprehensive. While many try to treat the condition with ear drops only, this is the most common cause of treatment failure. Ear drops cause the mites to simply move out of the ears and as far away as possible (usually to the base of the tail) until the insecticide levels in the ears drop to an acceptable level—then it's back to business as usual! The successful treatment of ear mites requires treating all animals in the household with a systemic insecticide, such as selamectin, or a combination of miticidal ear drops combined with whole-body flea-control preparations.

Demodicosis, sometimes referred to as red mange, can be one of the most difficult forms of mange to treat. Part of the problem has to do with the fact that the mites live in the hair follicles and they are relatively well shielded from topical and systemic products. The main issue, however, is that demodectic mange typically results only when there is some underlying process interfering with the dog's immune system.

Since *Demodex* mites are

normal residents of the skin of mammals, including humans, there is usually a mite population explosion only when the immune system fails to keep the number of mites in check. In young animals, the immune deficit may be transient or may reflect an actual inherited immune problem. In older animals, demodicosis is usually seen only when there is another disease hampering the immune system, such as diabetes, cancer, thyroid problems or the use of immune-suppressing drugs. Accordingly, treatment involves not only trying to kill the mange mites but also discerning what is interfering with immune function and correcting it if possible.

Chiggers represent several different species of mite that don't parasitize dogs specifically, but do latch on to passersby and can cause irritation. The problem is most prevalent in wooded areas in the late summer and fall. Treatment is not difficult, as the mites do not complete their life cycle on dogs and are susceptible to a variety of miticidal products.

MOSQUITOES

Mosquitoes have long been known to transmit a variety of diseases to people, as well as just being biting pests during warm weather. They also pose a real risk to pets. Not only do they carry deadly heartworms but recently there also has been much concern over their involvement with West Nile virus. While we can avoid heartworm with the use of preventive medications, there are no such preventives for West Nile virus. The only method of prevention in endemic areas is active mosquito control. Fortunately, most dogs that have been exposed to the virus only developed flu-like symptoms and, to date, there have not been the large number of reported deaths in canines as seen in some other species.

Illustration of *Demodex folliculoram*.

ILLUSTRATION BY PHOTOTAKE

MOSQUITO REPELLENT

Low concentrations of DEET (less than 10%), found in many human mosquito repellents, have been safely used in dogs but, in these concentrations, probably give only about two hours of protection. DEET may be safe in these small concentrations, but since it is not licensed for use on dogs, there is no research proving its safety for dogs. Products containing permethrin give the longest-lasting protection, perhaps two to four weeks. As DEET is not licensed for use on dogs, and both DEET and permethrin can be quite toxic to cats, appropriate care should be exercised. Other products, such as those containing oil of citronella, also have some mosquito-repellent activity, but typically have a relatively short duration of action.

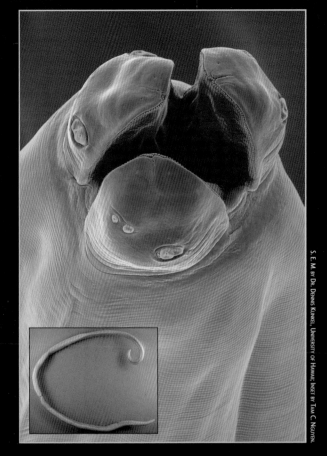

S. E. M. BY DR. DENNIS KUNKEL, UNIVERSITY OF HAWAII. INSET BY TAM C. NGUYEN.

The ascarid roundworm *Toxocara canis,* showing the mouth with three lips. INSET: Photomicrograph of the roundworm *Ascaris lumbricoides.*

INTERNAL PARASITES: WORMS

ASCARIDS

Ascarids are intestinal roundworms that rarely cause severe disease in dogs. Nonetheless, they are of major public health significance because they can be transferred to people. Sadly, it is children who are most commonly affected by the parasite, probably from inadvertently ingesting ascarid-contaminated soil. In fact, many yards and children's sandboxes contain appreciable numbers of ascarid eggs. So, while ascarids don't bite dogs or latch onto their intestines to suck blood, they do cause some nasty medical conditions in children and are best eradicated from our furry friends. Because pups can start passing ascarid eggs by three weeks of age, most parasite-control programs begin at two weeks of age and are repeated every two weeks until pups are eight weeks old. It is important to

HOOKED ON ANCYLOSTOMA

Adult dogs can become infected by the bloodsucking nematodes we commonly call hookworms via ingesting larvae from the ground or via the larvae penetrating the dog's skin. It is not uncommon for infected dogs to show no symptoms of hookworm infestation. Sometimes symptoms occur within ten days of exposure. These symptoms can include bloody diarrhea, anemia, loss of weight and general weakness. Dogs pass the hookworm eggs in their stools, which serves as the vet's method of identifying the infestation. The hookworm larvae can encyst themselves in the dog's tissues and be released when the dog is experiencing stress.

Caused by an *Ancylostoma* species whose common host is the dog, cutaneous larval migrans affects humans, causing itching and lumps and streaks beneath the surface of the skin.

S. E. M. BY DR. DENNIS KUNKEL, UNIVERSITY OF HAWAII.

realize that bitches can pass ascarids to their pups even if they test negative prior to whelping. Accordingly, bitches are best treated at the same time as the pups.

HOOKWORMS

Unlike ascarids, hookworms do latch onto a dog's intestinal tract and can cause significant loss of blood and protein. Similar to ascarids, hookworms can be transmitted to humans, where they cause a condition known as cutaneous larval migrans. Dogs can become infected either by consuming the infective larvae or by the larvae's penetrating the skin directly. People most often get infected when they are lying on the ground (such as on a beach) and the larvae penetrate the skin. Yes, the larvae can penetrate through a beach blanket. Hookworms are typically susceptible to the same medications used to treat ascarids.

The hookworm *Ancylostoma caninum* infests the intestines of dogs. INSET: Note the row of hooks at the posterior end, used to anchor the worm to the intestinal wall.

WHIPWORMS

Whipworms latch onto the lower aspects of the dog's colon and can cause cramping and diarrhea. Eggs do not start to appear in the dog's feces until about three months after the dog was infected. This worm has a peculiar life cycle, which makes it more difficult to control than ascarids or hookworms. The good thing is that whipworms rarely are transferred to people.

Some of the medications used to treat ascarids and hookworms are also effective against whipworms, but, in general, a separate treatment protocol is needed. Since most of the medications are effective against the adults but not the eggs or larvae, treatment is typically repeated in three weeks, and then often in three

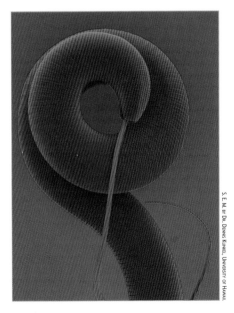

Adult whipworm, *Trichuris* sp., an intestinal parasite.

S. E. M. BY DR. DENNIS KUNKEL, UNIVERSITY OF HAWAII.

WORM-CONTROL GUIDELINES

- Practice sanitary habits with your dog and home.
- Clean up after your dog and don't let him sniff or eat other dogs' droppings.
- Control insects and fleas in the dog's environment. Fleas, lice, cockroaches, beetles, mice and rats can act as hosts for various worms.
- Prevent dogs from eating uncooked meat, raw poultry and dead animals.
- Keep dogs and children from playing in sand and soil.
- Kennel dogs on cement or gravel; avoid dirt runs.
- Administer heartworm preventives regularly.
- Have your vet examine your dog's stools at your annual visits.
- Select a boarding kennel carefully so as to avoid contamination from other dogs or an unsanitary environment.
- Prevent dogs from roaming. Obey local leash laws.

months as well. Unfortunately, since dogs don't develop resistance to whipworms, it is difficult to prevent them from getting reinfected if they visit soil contaminated with whipworm eggs.

TAPEWORMS

There are many different species of tapeworm that affect dogs, but *Dipylidium caninum* is probably the most common and is spread by fleas. Flea larvae feed on organic debris and tapeworm eggs in the environment and, when a dog chews at himself and manages to ingest fleas, he might get a dose of tapeworm at the same time. The tapeworm then develops further in the intestine of the dog.

The tapeworm itself, which is a parasitic flatworm that latches onto the intestinal wall, is composed of numerous segments. When the segments break off into the intestine (as proglottids), they may accumulate around the rectum, like grains of rice. While this tapeworm is disgusting in its behavior, it is not directly communicable to humans (although humans can also get infected by swallowing fleas).

A much more dangerous flatworm is *Echinococcus multilocularis*, which is typically found in foxes, coyotes and wolves. The eggs are passed in the feces and infect rodents, and, when dogs eat the rodents, the dogs can be infected by thousands of adult tapeworms. While the parasites don't cause many problems in dogs, this is considered the most lethal worm infection that people can get. Take appropriate precautions if you live in an area in which these tapeworms are found. Do not use mulch that may contain feces of dogs, cats or wildlife, and

discourage your pets from hunting wildlife. Treat these tapeworm infections aggressively in pets, because if humans get infected, approximately half die.

HEARTWORMS

Heartworm disease is caused by the parasite *Dirofilaria immitis* and is seen in dogs around the world. A member of the roundworm group, it is spread between dogs by the bite of an infected mosquito. The mosquito injects infective larvae into the dog's skin with its bite, and these larvae develop under the skin for a period of time before making their way to the heart. There they develop into adults, which grow and create blockages of the heart, lungs and major blood vessels there. They also start producing offspring (microfilariae),

S. E. M. by Dr. Dennis Kunkel, University of Hawaii.

A dog tapeworm proglottid (body segment).

S. E. M. by Dr. Dennis Kunkel, University of Hawaii.

The dog tapeworm *Taenia pisiformis*.

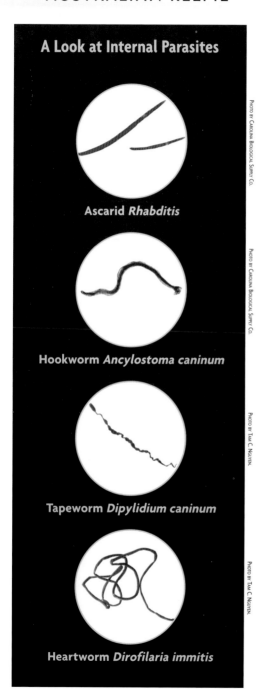

A Look at Internal Parasites

Ascarid *Rhabditis*

Hookworm *Ancylostoma caninum*

Tapeworm *Dipylidium caninum*

Heartworm *Dirofilaria immitis*

PHOTO BY CAROLINA BIOLOGICAL SUPPLY CO.

PHOTO BY CAROLINA BIOLOGICAL SUPPLY CO.

PHOTO BY TAM C. NGUYEN

PHOTO BY TAM C. NGUYEN

and these microfilariae circulate in the bloodstream, waiting to hitch a ride when the next mosquito bites. Once in the mosquito, the microfilariae develop into infective larvae and the entire process is repeated.

When dogs get infected with heartworm, over time they tend to develop symptoms associated with heart disease, such as coughing, exercise intolerance and potentially many other manifestations. Diagnosis is confirmed by either seeing the microfilariae themselves in blood samples or using immunologic tests (antigen testing) to identify the presence of adult heartworms. Since antigen tests measure the presence of adult heartworms and microfilarial tests measure offspring produced by adults, neither are positive until six to seven months after the initial infection. However, the beginning of damage can occur by fifth-stage larvae as early as three months after infection. Thus it is possible for dogs to be harboring problem-causing larvae for up to three months before either type of test would identify an infection.

The good news is that there are great protocols available for preventing heartworm in dogs. Testing is critical in the process, and it is important to understand the benefits as well as the limitations of such testing. All dogs six months of age or older that have not been on continuous heartworm-preventive medication

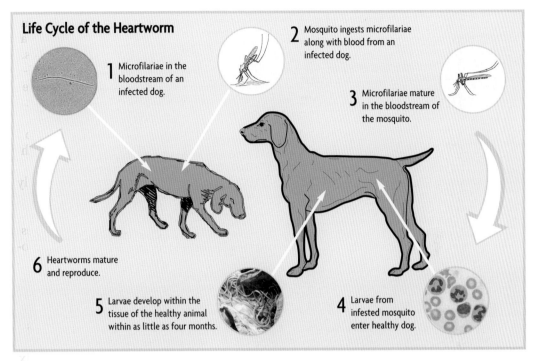

Life Cycle of the Heartworm

1 Microfilariae in the bloodstream of an infected dog.

2 Mosquito ingests microfilariae along with blood from an infected dog.

3 Microfilariae mature in the bloodstream of the mosquito.

4 Larvae from infested mosquito enter healthy dog.

5 Larvae develop within the tissue of the healthy animal within as little as four months.

6 Heartworms mature and reproduce.

should be screened with microfilarial or antigen tests. For dogs receiving preventive medication, periodic antigen testing helps assess the effectiveness of the preventives. The American Heartworm Society guidelines suggest that annual retesting may not be necessary when owners have absolutely provided continuous heartworm prevention. Retesting on a two- to three-year interval may be sufficient in these cases. However, your veterinarian will likely have specific guidelines under which heartworm preventives will be prescribed, and many prefer to err on the side of safety and retest annually.

It is indeed fortunate that heartworm is relatively easy to prevent, because treatments can be as life-threatening as the disease itself. Treatment requires a two-step process that kills the adult heartworms first and then the microfilariae. Prevention is obviously preferable; this involves a once-monthly oral or topical treatment. The most common oral preventives include ivermectin (not suitable for some breeds), moxidectin and milbemycin oxime; the once-a-month topical drug selamectin provides heartworm protection in addition to flea, some type of tick and other parasite controls.

THE ABCs OF
Emergency Care

Abrasions
Clean wound with running water or 3% hydrogen peroxide. Pat dry with gauze and spray with antibiotic. Do not cover.

Animal Bites
Clean area with soap and saline solution or water. Apply pressure to any bleeding area. Apply antibiotic ointment.

Antifreeze Poisoning
Induce vomiting and take dog to the vet.

Bee Sting
Remove stinger and apply soothing lotion or cold compress; give antihistamine in proper dosage.

Bleeding
Apply pressure directly to wound with gauze or towel for five to ten minutes. If wound does not stop bleeding, wrap wound with gauze and adhesive tape.

Bloat/Gastric Torsion
Immediately take the dog to the vet or emergency clinic; phone from car. No time to waste.

Burns
Chemical: Bathe dog with water and pet shampoo. Rinse in saline solution. Apply antibiotic ointment.

Acid: Rinse with water. Apply one part baking soda, two parts water to affected area.

Alkali: Rinse with water. Apply one part vinegar, four parts water to affected area.

Electrical: Apply antibiotic ointment. Seek veterinary assistance immediately.

Choking
If the dog is on the verge of collapsing, wedge a solid object, such as the handle of a screwdriver, between molars on one side of the mouth to keep mouth open. Pull tongue out. Use long-nosed pliers or fingers to remove foreign object. Do not push the object down the dog's throat. For small or medium dogs, hold dog upside down by hind legs and shake firmly to dislodge foreign object.

Chlorine Ingestion
With clean water, rinse the mouth and eyes. Give the dog water to drink; contact the vet.

Constipation
Feed dog 2 tablespoons bran flakes with each meal. Encourage drinking water. Mix 1/4-teaspoon mineral oil in dog's food.

Diarrhea
Withhold food for 12 to 24 hours. Feed dog antidiarrheal with eyedropper. When feeding resumes, feed one part boiled hamburger, one part plain cooked rice, 1/4- to 3/4-cup four times daily.

Dog Bite
Snip away hair around puncture wound; clean with 3% hydrogen peroxide; apply tincture of iodine. If wound appears deep, take the dog to the vet.

Frostbite
Wrap the dog in a heavy blanket. Warm affected area with a warm bath for ten minutes. Red color to skin will return with circulation; if tissues are pale after 20 minutes, contact the vet.

Use a portable, durable container large enough to contain all items.

DOG OWNER'S FIRST-AID KIT

- ❑ **Gauze bandages/swabs**
- ❑ **Adhesive and non-adhesive bandages**
- ❑ **Antibiotic powder**
- ❑ **Antiseptic wash**
- ❑ **Hydrogen peroxide 3%**
- ❑ **Antibiotic ointment**
- ❑ **Lubricating jelly**
- ❑ **Rectal thermometer**
- ❑ **Nylon muzzle**
- ❑ **Scissors and forceps**
- ❑ **Eyedropper**
- ❑ **Syringe**
- ❑ **Anti-bacterial/fungal solution**
- ❑ **Saline solution**
- ❑ **Antihistamine**
- ❑ **Cotton balls**
- ❑ **Nail clippers**
- ❑ **Screwdriver/pen knife**
- ❑ **Flashlight**
- ❑ **Emergency phone numbers**

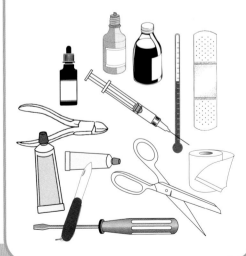

Heat Stroke
Partially submerge the dog in cold water to lower his body temperature while contacting the veterinarian.

Hot Spots
Mix 2 packets Domeboro® with 2 cups water. Saturate cloth with mixture and apply to hot spots for 15 to 30 minutes. Apply antibiotic ointment. Repeat every six to eight hours.

Poisonous Plants
Wash affected area with soap and water. Cleanse with alcohol. For foxtail/grass, apply antibiotic ointment.

Rat Poison Ingestion
Induce vomiting. Keep dog calm, maintain dog's normal body temperature (use blanket or heating pad). Get to the vet for antidote.

Shock
Keep the dog calm and warm; call for veterinary assistance.

Snake Bite
If possible, bandage the area and apply pressure. If the area is not conducive to bandaging, use ice to control bleeding. Get immediate help from the vet.

Tick Removal
Apply flea and tick spray directly on tick. Wait one minute. Using tweezers or wearing plastic gloves, apply constant pull while grasping tick's body. Apply antibiotic ointment.

Vomiting
Restrict dog's water intake; offer a few ice cubes. Withhold food for next meal. Contact vet if vomiting persists longer than 24 hours.

AUSTRALIAN KELPIE

Kelpies are ever young, or so say their many adoring fans. Who could imagine his full-of-energy Kelpie "kid" ever slowing down? Just like humans, dogs grow old, much to our regret and sadness, but veterinary science has made wonderful advances in lengthening the lifespans of our dogs. Just as humans more commonly live to be 90 or better today, more dogs are living well into their teens; a 20-year-old dog is not unheard of! The Australian Kelpie is fortunate to enjoy a life expectancy of about 13 years, some even older. For comparison purposes, that likens a 13-year-old Kelpie to an 80-year-old human; thus the old "7 dog years to 1 human year" theory is not accurate. There is no hard and fast rule for comparing dog and human ages.

SIGNS OF AGING

By the time your dog has reached his senior years, you will know him very well, so the physical and behavioral changes that accompany aging should be noticeable to you. An obvious physical sign of aging is gray hair. Graying often occurs first on the muzzle and face, around the eyes. Other telltale signs are the dog's overall decrease in activity. Your older dog might be more content to nap and rest, and he may not show the same old enthusiasm for activity. Other physical signs include significant weight loss or gain; more labored movement; skin and coat problems, possibly hair loss; sight and/or hearing problems; changes in toileting habits, perhaps seeming "unhousebroken" at times; and tooth decay, bad breath or other mouth problems.

There are behavioral changes that go along with aging, too. There are numerous causes for behavioral changes. Sometimes a dog's apparent confusion results from a physical change like diminished sight or hearing. If his confusion causes him to be afraid, he may act aggressively or defensively. He may sleep more frequently because his daily walks, though shorter now, tire him out. He may begin to experience separation anxiety or, conversely, become less interested in petting and attention.

There also are clinical conditions that cause behavioral changes in older dogs. One such condition is known as canine cognitive dysfunction (familiarly known as "old-dog" syndrome). It can be frustrating for an owner whose dog is affected with cognitive dysfunction, as it can result in behavioral changes of all types, most seemingly unexplainable. Common changes include the dog's forgetting aspects of the daily routine, such as times to eat, go out for walks, relieve himself and the like. Along the same lines, you may take your dog out at the regular time for a potty trip and he may have no idea why he is there. Sometimes a placid dog will begin to show aggressive or possessive tendencies or, conversely, a hyperactive dog will start to "mellow out."

Disease also can be the cause of behavioral changes in senior dogs. Hormonal problems (Cushing's disease is common in older dogs), diabetes and thyroid disease can cause increased appetite, which can lead to aggression related to food guarding. It's better to be proactive with your senior dog, making more frequent trips to the vet if necessary and having bloodwork done to test for the diseases that can commonly befall older dogs.

The aforementioned changes are discussed to alert owners to the things that *may* happen as their dogs get older. Many hardy dogs remain active and alert well into old age. However, it can be frustrating and heartbreaking for owners to see their beloved dogs change physically and temperamentally. Just know that it's the same Australian Kelpie under there

Humans aren't the only ones to go gray. A gray muzzle and face are outward indicators of a dog's advanced age.

and that he still loves you and appreciates your care, which he needs now more than ever.

CARING FOR MY AGING DOG

Again, every dog is an individual in terms of aging. Your dog might advance in years and show no signs of slowing down. However, even if he shows no outward signs of aging, he should begin a senior-care program as determined by your vet. By providing him with extra attention to his veterinary care at this age, you will be practicing good preventive medicine, ensuring that the rest of your dog's life will be as long, active, happy and healthy as possible. If you do notice indications of aging, such as graying and/or changes in sleeping, eating or toileting habits, this is a sign to set up a senior-care visit with your vet right away to make sure that these changes are not related to any health problems.

To start, senior dogs should visit the vet twice yearly for exams, routine tests and overall evaluations. Many veterinarians have special screening programs especially for senior dogs that can include a thorough physical exam; blood test to determine complete blood count; serum biochemistry test, which screens for liver, kidney and blood problems as well as cancer; urinalysis; and dental exams. With these tests, it can be determined whether your dog has any health problems; the results also establish a baseline for your pet against which future test results can be compared.

In addition to these tests, your vet may suggest additional testing, including an EKG, tests for glaucoma and other problems of the eye, chest x-rays, screening for tumors, blood pressure test, test for thyroid function and screening for parasites and reassessment of his preventive program. Your vet also will ask you questions about your dog's diet and activity level, what you feed and the amounts that you feed to determine if a change is needed. This may seem like quite a work-up for your pet, but veterinarians advise that older dogs need more frequent attention so that any health problems can be detected as early as possible. Serious conditions like kidney disease, heart disease and cancer may not present outward symptoms, or the problem may go undetected if the symptoms are mistaken by owners as just part of the aging process.

There are some conditions

more common in elderly dogs that are difficult to ignore. Cognitive dysfunction shares much in common with senility and Alzheimer's disease, and dogs are not immune. Be heartened by the fact that, in some ways, there are more treatment options for dogs with cognitive dysfunction than for people with similar conditions. There is good evidence that continued stimulation in the form of games, play, training and exercise can help to maintain cognitive function. There are also medications (such as seligiline) and antioxidant-fortified senior diets that have been shown to be beneficial.

Cancer is also a condition more common in the elderly. Almost all of the cancers seen in people are also seen in pets. If pets are getting regular physical examinations, cancers are often detected early. There are a variety of cancer therapies available today, and many pets continue to live happy lives with appropriate treatment.

Degenerative joint disease, often referred to as arthritis, is another malady common to both elderly dogs and humans. A lifetime of wear and tear on the joints eventually takes its toll and results in stiffness and difficulty in getting around. Hopefully your pet has not been carrying extra pounds and wearing those joints out before their time. If your pet was unfortunate enough to inherit hip dysplasia, osteochondritis dissecans or any of the other developmental orthopedic diseases, battling the onset of degenerative joint disease was probably a longstanding goal. In any case, there are now many effective remedies for managing degenerative joint disease and a number of remarkable surgeries as well.

Aside from the extra veterinary care, there is much you can do at home to keep your older dog in good condition. The dog's diet is an important factor. If your dog's appetite decreases, he will not be getting the nutrients he needs. He also will lose weight, which is unhealthy for a dog at a proper weight. Conversely, an older dog's metabolism is slower and he usually exercises less, but he should not be allowed to become obese. Obesity in an older dog is especially risky, because extra pounds mean extra stress on the body, increasing his vulnerability to heart disease. Additionally, the extra pounds make it harder for the dog to move about. You should discuss age-related feeding changes with your vet.

As for exercise, the senior dog should not be allowed to become a "couch potato" despite his old age. Your Kelpie needs to get up and get moving based on what he is capable of, so let your dog set the pace. Many dogs remain active in their senior years, so base changes to the exercise program on your own individual dog. Don't worry, your Kelpie will let you know when it's time to rest.

Keep up with your grooming routine as you always have. Be extra-diligent about checking the skin and coat for problems. Older dogs can experience thinning coats as a normal aging process, but they can also lose hair as a result of medical problems. Some thinning is normal, but patches of baldness or the loss of significant amounts of hair is not.

Hopefully, you've been regular with brushing your dog's teeth throughout his life. Healthy teeth directly affect overall good health. We already know that bacteria from gum infections can enter the dog's body through the damaged gums and travel to the organs. At a stage in life when his organs don't function as well as they used to, you don't want anything to put additional strain on them. Clean teeth also contribute to a healthy immune system. Offering the dental-type chews in addition to toothbrushing can help, as they remove plaque and tartar as the dog chews.

Along with the same good care you've given him all of his life, pay a little extra attention to your dog in his senior years and keep up with twice-yearly trips to the vet. The sooner a problem is uncovered, the greater the chances of a full recovery.

UNDERSTANDING THE CANINE MINDSET

For starters, you and your dog are on different wavelengths. Your dog is similar to a toddler in that both live in the present tense only. A dog's view of life is based primarily on cause and effect. Your dog makes connections based on the fact that he lives in the present, so when he is doing something and you interrupt to dispense praise or a correction, a connection, positive or negative, is made. To the dog, that's like one plus one equals two! In the same sense, it's also easy to see that when your timing is off, you will cause an incorrect connection. The one-plus-one way of thinking is why you must never scold a dog for behavior that took place an hour, 15 minutes or even 5 seconds ago. But it is also why, when your timing is perfect, you can teach him to do all kinds of wonderful things—as soon as he has made that essential connection. What helps the process is his desire to please you and to have your approval.

There are behaviors we admire in dogs, such as friendliness and obedience, as well as those behaviors that cause problems to a varying degree. The dog owner who encounters minor behavioral problems is wise to solve them promptly or get professional help. Bad behaviors are not corrected by repeatedly shouting "No" or getting angry with the dog. Only the giving of praise and approval for good behavior lets your dog understand right from wrong. The longer a bad behavior is allowed to continue, the harder it is to overcome. A responsible breeder is often able to help. Each dog is unique, so try not to compare your dog's behavior with your neighbor's dog or the one you had as a child.

Have your veterinarian check the dog to see whether a behavior problem could have a physical cause. An earache or toothache, for example, could be the reason for a dog to snap at you if you were to touch his head when putting on his leash. A sharp correction from you would only increase the behavior. When a physical basis is eliminated, and if the problem is not something you understand or can cope with, ask for the name of a behavioral specialist, preferably one who is familiar with the Kelpie. Be sure to keep the breeder informed of your progress.

Many things, such as environment and inherited traits, form the basic behavior of a dog, just as in humans. You also must factor into your Kelpie's temperament the purpose for which your dog was originally bred—herding and a hard day's work. The major obstacle lies in the dog's inability to explain his behavior to us in a way that we understand. The one thing you should not do is to give up and abandon your dog. Somewhere a misunderstanding has occurred but, with help and

Whether used for their intended purpose or not, the breed's instincts remain strong in Kelpies. This dog exhibits typical herding movements.

patient understanding on your part, you should be able to work out the majority of bothersome behaviors.

AGGRESSION

"Aggression" is a word that is often misunderstood and is sometimes even used to describe what is actually normal canine behavior. For example, it's normal for puppies to growl when playing tug-of-war. It's puppy talk. There are different forms of dog aggression, but all are degrees of dominance, indicating that the dog, not his master, is (or thinks he is) in control. When the dog feels that he (or his control of the situation) is threatened, he will respond. The Kelpie is typically a non-aggressive breed, but in any breed aggressive behavior varies with individual dogs. It is not at all pleasant to see bared teeth or to hear your dog growl or snarl, but these are signs of behavior that, if left uncorrected, can become extremely dangerous. A word of

DOMINANCE

Dogs are born with dominance skills, meaning that they can be quite clever in trying to get their way. The "follow-me" trot to the cookie jar is an example. The toy dropped in your lap says "Play with me." The leash delivered to you along with an excited look means "Take me for a walk." These are all good-natured dominant behaviors. Ask your dog to sit before agreeing to his request and you'll remain "top dog."

warning here: never challenge an aggressive dog. He is unpredictable and therefore unreliable to approach.

Nothing gets a "hello" from strangers on the street quicker than walking a puppy, but people should ask permission before petting your dog so you can tell him to sit in order to receive the admiring pats. If a hand comes down over the dog's head and he shrinks back, ask the person to bring his hand up, underneath the pup's chin. Now you're correcting strangers, too! But if you don't, it could make your dog afraid of strangers, which in turn can lead to fear biting. Socialization prevents much aggression before it rears its ugly head.

The body language of an aggressive dog about to attack is clear. The dog will have a hard, steady stare. He will try to look as big as possible by standing stiff-legged, pushing out his chest, keeping his ears up and holding his tail up and steady. The hackles on his back will rise so that a ridge of hairs stands up. This posture may include the curled lip, snarl and/or growl, or he may be silent. He looks, and definitely is, very dangerous.

This dominant posture is seen in dogs that are territorially aggressive. Deliverymen are constant victims of serious bites from such dogs. Territorial aggression is the reason you should never, ever try to train a puppy to be a watchdog. It can escalate into this type of behavior over which you will have no control. All forms of aggression must be taken seriously and dealt with immediately. If signs of aggressive behavior continue, or grow worse, or if you are at all unsure about how to deal with your dog's behavior, get the help of a professional.

Uncontrolled aggression, sometimes called "irritable aggression," is not something for the pet owner to try to solve. If you cannot solve your dog's dangerous behavior with professional help, and you (quite rightly) do not wish to keep a canine time-bomb in your home, you will have some important decisions to make. Aggressive dogs often cannot be rehomed successfully, as they are dangerous and unreliable in their behavior. An aggressive dog should be dealt with only by someone who knows the breed, knows exactly the situation that he is getting into and has the experience, dedication and ideal living environment to attempt rehabilitating the dog. In cases where rehabilitation is not possible, the dog ends up having to be humanely put down. Making a decision about euthanasia is not an easy undertaking for anyone, for any reason, but you cannot pass on to another home a dog that you know could cause harm.

A milder form of aggression is the dog's guarding anything that he perceives to be his—his food dish, his toys, his bed and/or his crate. This can be prevented if you take firm control from the start. The young puppy can and should be taught that his leader will share, but that certain rules apply. Guarding is mild aggression only in the beginning stages, and it will worsen and become dangerous if you let it.

Don't try to snatch anything away from your puppy. Bargain for the item in question so that you can positively reinforce him when he gives it up. Punishment only results in worsening any aggressive behavior.

Many dogs extend their guarding impulse toward items they've stolen. The dog figures, "If I have it, it's mine!" (Some ill-behaved kids have similar tendencies.) An angry confrontation will only increase the dog's aggression. (Have you ever watched a child have a tantrum?) Try a simple distraction first, such as tossing a toy or picking up his leash for a walk. If that doesn't work, the best way to handle the situation is with basic obedience. Show the dog a treat, followed by calm, almost slow-motion commands: "Come. Sit. Drop it. Good dog," and then hand over the cheese! That's one example of positive-reinforcement training.

Children can be bitten when they try to retrieve a stolen shoe or toy, so they need to know how to handle the dog or to let an adult do it. They may also be bitten as they run away from a dog, in either fear or play. The dog sees the child's running as reason for pursuit, and even a friendly young puppy will nip at the heels of a runaway. Teach the kids not to run away from a strange dog and when to stop overly exciting play with their own puppy.

Fear biting is yet another aggressive behavior. A fear biter gives many warning signals. The dog leans away from the approaching person (sometimes hiding behind his owner) with his ears and tail down, but not in submission. He may even shiver. His hackles are raised, his lips curled. When the person steps into the dog's "flight zone" (a circle of 1 to 3 feet surrounding the dog), he attacks. Because of the fear factor, he performs a rapid attack-and-retreat. Because it is directed at a person, vets are often the victims of this form of aggression. It is frightening, but discovering and eliminating the cause of the fright will help overcome the dog's need to bite. Early socialization again plays a strong role in the prevention of this behavior. Again, if you can't cope with it, get the help of an expert.

MATTERS OF SEX

For whatever reasons, real or imagined, most people tend to have a preference in choosing between a male and female puppy. Some, but not all, of the undesirable traits attributed to the sex of the dog can be

Playtime with other dogs, young and old, usually includes wrestling and roughhousing, not to be confused with aggressive behavior.

suppressed by early spaying or neutering. The major advantage, of course, is that a neutered male or a spayed female will not be adding to the overpopulation of dogs.

An unaltered male will mark territory by lifting his leg everywhere, leaving a few drops of urine indoors on your furniture and appliances and outside on everything he passes. It is difficult to catch him in the act, because he leaves only a few drops each time, but it is very hard to eliminate the odor. Thus the cycle begins, because the odor will entice him to mark that spot again.

If you have bought a bitch with the intention of breeding her, be sure you know what you are getting into. She will go through one or two periods of estrus each year, each cycle lasting about three weeks. During those times she will have to be kept confined to protect your furniture and to protect her from being bred by a male other than the one you have selected. Breeding should never be undertaken to "show the kids the miracle of birth." Bitches can die giving birth, and the puppies may also die. The dam often exhibits what is called "maternal aggression" after the pups are born. Her intention is to protect her pups, but in fact she can be extremely vicious. Breeding should be left to the experienced breeders, who do so for the betterment of the breed and with much research and planning behind each mating.

Mounting is not unusual in dogs, male or female. Puppies do it to each other and adults do it regardless of sex, because it is not so much a sexual act as it is one of dominance. It becomes very annoying when the dog mounts your legs, the kids or the couch cushions; in these and any other instances of mounting, he should be corrected. Touching sometimes stimulates the dog, so pulling the dog off by his collar or leash, together with a consistent and stern "Off!" command, usually eliminates the behavior.

CHEWING

All puppies chew. All dogs chew. This is a fact of life for canines, and sometimes you may think it's what your dog does best! A pup starts chewing when his first set of teeth erupts and continues throughout the teething period. Chewing gives the pup relief from itchy gums and incoming teeth and, from that time on, he gets great satisfaction out of this normal, somewhat idle, canine activity. Providing safe chew toys is the best way to direct this behavior in an appropriate manner. Chew toys are available in all sizes, textures and flavors, but you must monitor the wear-

When it comes to chewing, Kelpie pups aren't afraid of a challange!

and-tear inflicted on your pup's toys to be sure that the ones you've chosen are safe and remain in good condition.

Puppies cannot distinguish between a rawhide toy and a nice leather shoe or wallet. It's up to you to keep your possessions away from the dog and to keep your eye on the dog. There's a form of destruction caused by chewing that is not the dog's fault. Let's say you allow him on the sofa. One day he takes a rawhide bone up on the sofa and, in the course of chewing on the bone, takes up a bit of fabric. He continues to chew. Disaster! Now you've learned the lesson: dogs with chew toys have to be either kept off furniture and carpets, carefully supervised or put into their confined areas for chew time.

The wooden legs of furniture are favorite objects for chewing. The first time, tell the dog "Leave it!" (or "No!") and offer him a chew toy as a substitute. But your clever dog may be hiding under the chair and doing some silent destruction, which you may not notice until it's too late. In this case, it's time to try one of the foul-tasting products, made specifically to prevent destructive chewing, that is sprayed on the objects of your dog's chewing attention. These products also work to keep the dog away from plants, trash, etc. It's even a good way to stop the dog from "mouthing" or chewing on your hands or the leg of your pants. (Be sure to wash your hands after the mouthing lesson!) A little spray goes a long way.

DIGGING

Digging is another natural and normal canine behavior. Wild canines dig to bury whatever food they can save for later to eat. (And you thought *we* invented the doggie bag!) Burying bones or toys is a primary cause to dig. Dogs also dig to get at interesting little underground creatures like moles and mice. In the summer, they dig to get down to cool earth. In winter, they dig to get beneath the cold surface to warmer earth.

The solution to the last two is easy. In the summer, provide a bed that's up off the ground and placed in a shaded area. In winter, the dog should either be indoors to sleep or given an adequate insulated doghouse outdoors. To understand how natural and

> **GIMME WHEELS!**
> Chasing cars or bikes is dangerous for all parties concerned: dogs, drivers and cyclists. Something about those wheels going around fascinates dogs, but that fascination can end in disastrous results. Corrections for your dog's chasing behavior must be immediate and firm. Tell him "Leave it!" and then give him either a sit or a down command. Get kids on bikes to help saturate your dog with spinning wheels while he politely practices his sits and downs.

normal this is you have only to consider the Nordic breeds of sled dog who, at the end of the run, routinely dig a bed for themselves in the snow. It's the nesting instinct. How often have you seen your dog go round and round in circles, pawing at his blanket or bedding before flopping down to sleep?

Domesticated dogs also dig to escape, and that's a lot more dangerous than it is destructive. A dog that digs under the fence is the one that is hit by a car or becomes lost. A good fence to protect a digger should be set 10 to 12 inches below ground level, and every fence needs to be routinely checked for even the smallest openings that can become possible escape routes.

Catching your dog in the act of digging is the easiest way to stop it, because your dog will make the "one-plus-one" connection, but digging is too often a solitary occupation, something the lonely dog does out of boredom. Catch your young puppy in the act and put a stop to it before you have a yard full of craters. It is more difficult to stop if your dog sees you gardening. If you can dig, why can't he? Because you say so, that's why! Some dogs are excavation experts, and some dogs never dig. However, when it comes to any of these instinctive canine behaviors, never say "never."

JUMPING UP
Jumping up is a device of enthusiastic, attention-seeking puppies, but adult dogs often like to jump up as well, usually as a form of canine greeting. This is a controversial issue. Some owners wouldn't have it any other way! They encourage their dogs, and the owners and dogs alike enjoy the friendly physical contact. Some owners think that it's cute when it comes from a puppy but not from an adult.

Conversely, there are those who consider jumping up to be one of the worst kinds of bad manners to be found in a dog. Among this group inevitably are bound to be some of your best friends. There are two situations in which your dog should be restrained from any and all jumping up. One is around

While some canine behavior is frustrating, most of it is just plain entertaining.

children, especially young children and those who are not at ease with dogs. The other is when you are entertaining guests. No one who comes dressed up for a party wants to be groped by your dog, no matter how friendly his intentions or how clean his paws.

The answer to this one is relatively simple. If the dog has already started to jump up, the first command is "Off," followed immediately by "Sit." The dog must sit every time you are about to meet a friend on the street or when someone enters your home, be it child or adult. You may have to ask people to ignore the dog for a few minutes in order to let his urge for an enthusiastic greeting subside. If your dog is too exuberant and won't sit still, you'll have to work harder by first telling him "Off" and then issuing the down/stay command. This requires more work on your part, because the down is a submissive position and your dog is only trying to be super-friendly. A small treat is expected when training for this particular down.

If you have a real pet peeve about a dog's jumping up, then disallow it from the day your puppy comes home. Jumping up is a subliminally taught human-to-dog greeting. Dogs don't greet each other in this way. It begins because your puppy is close to the ground and he's easier to pet and cuddle if he reaches up and you bend over to meet him halfway. If you won't like it later, don't start it when he is young, but do give lots of praise and affection for a good sit.

BARKING

Here's a big, noisy problem! Telling a dog he must never bark is like telling a child not to speak! Consider how confusing it must be to your dog that you are using your voice (which is your form of barking) to teach him when to bark and when not to! That is precisely the reason not to "bark back" when the dog's barking is annoying you (or your neighbors). Try to understand the scenario from the dog's viewpoint. He barks. You bark. He barks again, you bark again. This "conversa-tion" can go on forever!

The first time your adorable little puppy said "Yip" or "Yap," you were ecstatic. His first word! You smiled, you told him how smart he was—and you allowed him to do it. So there's that one-plus-one thing again, because he will understand by your happy reaction that "Mr. Alpha loves it when I talk." Ignore his barking in the beginning, and allow it, but don't encourage barking during play. Instead, use the "put a toy in it" method to tone it down. Add a very soft "Quiet" as you hand off the toy. If the barking continues, stand up straight, fold your arms and turn your back on the dog. If he barks, you won't play, and you should follow the same rule for all undesirable behavior during play.

Dogs bark in reaction to sounds and sights. Another dog's bark, a person passing by or even just rustling leaves can set off a barker. If someone coming up your driveway or to your door provokes a barking frenzy, use the saturation method to stop it. Have several friends come and go every three or four minutes over as long a period of time as they can spare (it could take a couple of hours). Attach about a foot of rope to the dog's collar and have very small treats handy. Each time a car pulls up or a person approaches, let the dog bark once (grab the rope if you need to physically restrain him), say "Okay, good dog," give him a treat and make him sit. "Okay" is the release command. It lets the dog know that he has alerted you and tells him that you are now in charge. That person leaves and the next arrives and so on and so on until everyone—especially the dog—is bored and the barking has stopped. Don't forget to thank your friends. Your neighbors, by the way, may be more than willing to assist you in this parlor game.

Excessive barking outdoors is more difficult to keep in check because, when it happens, he is outside and you are probably inside. A few warning barks are fine, but use the same method to tell him when enough is enough. You will have to stay outside with him for that bit of training.

There is one more kind of vocalizing which is called "idiot barking" (from idiopathic, meaning of unknown cause). It is usually rhythmic or a timed series of barks. Put a stop to it immediately by calling the dog to come. This form of barking can drive neighbors crazy and commonly occurs when a dog is bored. With

STOP, THIEF!
The easiest way to prevent a dog from stealing food is to stop this behavior before it starts by never leaving food out where he can reach it. However, if it is too late, and your dog has already made a steal, you must stop your furry felon from becoming a repeat offender. Once Sneaky Pete has successfully stolen food, place a bit of food where he can reach it. Place an empty soda can with some pebbles in it on top the food. Leave the room and watch what happens. As the dog grabs the tasty morsel, the can comes with it. The noise of the tumbling pebble-filled can makes its own correction, and you don't have to say a word.

a Kelpie this should not be an issue because Kelpie owners know the importance of plenty of interesting activity for their dogs.

INDEX

My Australian Kelpie

PUT YOUR PUPPY'S FIRST PICTURE HERE

Dog's Name _____

Date _____ Photographer _____